THE TECHNIQUE OF

Decorative
Stained Glass

THE TECHNIQUE OF
Decorative
Stained Glass

Paul San Casciani

Dover Publications, Inc., New York

Library of Congress Cataloging-in-Publication Data

San Casciani, Paul.
    The technique of decorative stained glass/Paul San Casciani.
        p.   cm.
    Reprint. Originally published: London: B. T. Batsford, 1985.
    Bibliography: p.
    Includes index.
    ISBN 0-486-26157-3
    1. Glass craft.   2. Glass painting and staining—Patterns.
    I. Title.
    TT298.S26   1989
    748.5′028—dc20   89-32466
                                    CIP

Printed in Great Britain by The Bath Press, Avon

Acknowledgements

I would like to thank the following advisers for reading through sections of the text and for giving me valuable comments: Arthur Goodwin, Vice-Principal, Exeter College of Art & Design; David O'Connor, Lecturer in the History of Fine Art, Manchester University; John Duncan, Lecturer, College of Further Education, Oxford; Michelle Sykes, Lecturer to the Victoria and Albert Museum, London, and Organiser of the Education Service, Ashmolean Museum, Oxford, and Alfred Fisher, Chapel Studio, Watford.

All photographs, except for the credits given below, were taken by Keith Waters, Lecturer in Photography, Berkshire College of Art; I am grateful to him for his unstinting efforts and unfailing enthusiasm during our many photographic sessions. Other photographs are credited as follows: Figs. 3 and 4, Dave Crump; Figs. 21–24, Alun Thornton Jones; Fig. 33, Pilkington Glass Museum; Fig. 39, the Art Department, Dragon School, Oxford; Figs. 12 and 53, H. L. Harris; Figs. 55 and 58, Eric English; Fig. 56, David O'Connor; Fig. 57, William Cole, and Fig. 59, Victoria and Albert Museum (Crown Copyright).

Thanks go to Francis Skeat, for allowing me to show work in progress on his designs in Chapter 4, and also to Mr and Mrs Taylor-Ballentyne, for providing a photo of Elgar.

I would also like to mention the many students I have taught over the years, who have all contributed to my experience and, through their enthusiasm, helped to make this book possible.

Lastly, I thank my wife Paula for the generous help and encouragement she has given me in preparing all the notes and typing up the manuscript.

Contents

Preface

Stained glass has now become an umbrella term for a great variety of decorative techniques using coloured glass. Some techniques, such as leading and glasspainting, are traditional methods with a history of nearly 1000 years; but there are other techniques, such as copperfoil and fusing, developed this century, which are ideal for making decorative items.

In 1968 I was invited by the now retired Principal of the Marylebone Institute, London, Miss J. Adams, under the auspices of the Inner London Education Authority, to set up a practical stained glass evening class for the general public. I do not know of anywhere else in the country that was at that time making stained glass available to anyone with the enthusiasm to learn. The art school courses were available only to full-time students with qualifications; but I believed it was very important to offer a course to anyone who showed interest in this neglected medium. Since then I have had the satisfaction of seeing the 'glassroots' activities develop; and in recent years there has been a rapid acceleration of public enthusiasm for this beautiful art form. This has meant a beneficial result for professionals and non-professionals alike, because there is now an ever-growing range of materials and equipment being made available in this country.

The purpose of this book is to present a series of projects of carefully graded difficulty in each technique, based on my experience of teaching the general public for over sixteen years. The commonest fault in students is the tendency to want to rush ahead in their enthusiasm, without acquiring the proper grounding. Please use this book as it has been designed, and so gain a good basic training in various techniques. Patience in making the simple basic projects properly will pay dividends when tackling more difficult work.

In order not to intimidate the beginner, there is a tendency in some manuals to ignore standards. I would urge all those who take up making stained glass as an interest to be aware of the importance of standards and to do their best to produce well-crafted work. We should strive to contribute something to the medium, no matter how small.

I am well aware of the need to use materials and equipment as economically as possible, and the projects in the range of techniques outlined in this book will enable you to use up all your glass creatively – you need not throw away the tiniest scrap.

When making stained glass, you become part of a great tradition, changing and adapting to the demands of each epoch. The final chapter provides a brief outline of the history of stained glass, followed by a bibliography to which you may refer to deepen your understanding of the medium.

I am convinced that it is crucial to the future of stained glass in this country that many people become involved in it. We have a magnificent heritage of stained glass, mainly ecclesiastical, in our country, and we need to have an enlightened public keen to conserve all we have. We also have a tradition of decorative domestic panels, from the Victorian period through to the 1930s, which give character to a dwelling. People are now realising their value and are keen either to restore their examples or to reintroduce colourful panels into their homes; and, as this book demonstrates, stained glass can be an imaginative feature in any home. In addition, when people start making small decorative items of their own, they will want to see stained glass used in a larger context, and press for colourful examples in their local library or community centre, and be pleased to see it in restaurants, hotels and shops.

With the active interest of an enthusiastic and informed public, I believe that stained glass can be assured of a lively future.

CHAPTER ONE

Introduction to traditional leading

MATERIALS

Types of glass available (see Fig. 1)

Pieces of glass can be bought from stockists (seee p. 117). and, as the hobby market is developing, it is becoming usual for a standard cut size 204mm (8in) × 305mm (12in) to be available. This small size is obviously dearer than larger amounts, such as half stock sheets and full stock sheets. Full sheet sizes vary according to the type of glass and the manufacturer. Some stockists will sell you exactly the size you want, but for this service you will have to pay 20 per cent more, as they are left with the off-cuts.

Machine-made glass
This is the cheaper end of the market: very pale tints are the cheapest. Machine-made glass has been processed through rollers to give a standard thickness: 3mm ($\frac{1}{8}$in). It is often less translucent than hand-made glass because it usually has a slight texture on it. It is ideal for the beginner because it is easy to cut and relatively inexpensive.

In this category are waterglass (lightly rippled surface [11]); seedy (containing bubbles as a decorative feature); cathedral (clear but lightly textured); hammered (a lively texture); glue chip (frost-like patterns on surface [5]); wispy (opalescent on a cathedral base [3]), and iridescent (clear or wispy with different iridescent effects).

Cathedral glass, semi hand-made (8)
There is an attractive, semi hand-made type produced in England called streaky rolled cathedral. The individual colours, taken from pots of molten glass, are mixed by hand in a ladle and poured through rollers. Its colour is richer than the standard cathedral lines.

Opalescent glass, machine-made
This glass is a mixture of swirling opaque and translucent patterns in a wide variety of colours. It is popular for lamps and decorative items such as boxes, plant-pot holders, wall plaques and so on.

Hand-made glass
Opalescent glass, semi hand-made (1)   This English glass is manufactured in the same way as streaky rolled cathedral, but it is made partly opaque by the introduction of white opal. Its patterns are more individual and fantastic than those in machine-made opalescent.

Novelty glass (art glass)   The lively interest in unusual glasses in the USA has produced fascinating types: ring-mottled (7); semi-sculptural drapery glass (4); clear and opalescent ripples; fractures and streamers. Large stained glass stockists will have examples. They are costly, but very exciting to use.

'Antique' hand-made glass   This category is not old glass, but it is termed 'antique' because it is made in the medieval way: mouth-blown. The glass is blown into a muff (10) before it becomes a sheet (9); for the explanation of this process see p. 105.

Its colours are the richest of any glass, it has much more sparkle, and it is full of irregularities such as bubbles and streaks. Each sheet varies in tone from area to area and it is characteristically uneven in thickness. This glass is equivalent, in fabric terms, to raw silk or hand-woven cloth. All its irregularities are to be exploited as part of its beauty, for these 'imperfections' help to modify the light and give interest. 'Antique' hand-made glass which has the same colour all through its thickness is called pot metal glass. Another type of glass, which has a base glass laminated with a thin layer of a different colour, such as red on white, red on pale blue, or green on white, is known as 'flashed' glass, and can be used, for example, in heraldry, as the layer of

fig. 1 Various types of stained glass

diag. 1 Key to Fig. 1, numbered: 1 ★Streaky opalescent (English) 2 ★Bullion (spun glass/roundel/crown) 3 Wispy (American) 4 ★Drapery (American) 5 Glue chip (American) 6 Dalle-de-verre (English) 7 ★Ring mottled (American) 8 ★Streaky rolled cathedral (English) 9 ★'Antique' (English) 10 ★Muff 'antique' streaky (English) 11 Waterglass (American) 12 ★'Curious white' (English) ★ = (semi) hand-made

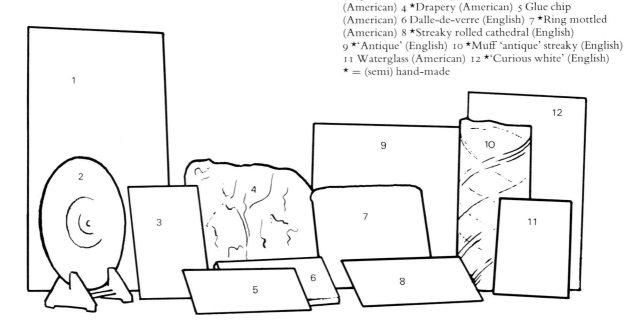

colour can be removed with hydrofluoric acid. Most reds (called 'ruby' in the trade) are flashed, except for selenium, an orange-red, and dalle-de-verre rubies.

In addition to these rich colours, 'antique' glass is also available in a variety of pale tints. Reamy glass has the effect of swirling movements in water; seedy has many bubbles, created by throwing a potato into the pot of molten glass (as it burns up it gives off oxygen which is trapped in the form of myriad tiny bubbles in the glass); whilst 'curious white' (12) has a more distinctive wavy patterning than reamy. Plain tinted whites have a yellow or a green bias and are often chosen for glasspainting projects.

Bullions (2) (also known as roundels, spun or crown glass)
These are mouth-blown spun discs of glass, available in various colours and sizes. For method of manufacture see p.105

Bevels
These are clear glass bevelled shapes available in various geometric designs; they are particularly attractive in door panels.

'Jewels'
These eye-catching small pieces of glass, often faceted, can be used in lamps to create focal points.

Dalle-de-verre (6)
This slab glass is usually about 25mm (1in) thick, to be set in concrete or resin. Broken pieces put in the kiln turn into 'globs' which can be used to appliqué surfaces.

Types of lead

A length of lead is called a 'calm'; many American books have modernised this spelling to 'came' or even 'cane', but I prefer to retain the old spelling which reminds us of its picturesque manufacture in medieval times. Molten lead was poured into a shallow wooden box lined with sand and containing reeds (Latin *calamus*). When the metal had cooled, the reeds were taken out, leaving long lead strips with an 'H' section where the reeds had been. A calm varies in length, averaging 1.52m (5ft) according to the size and manufacturer. All my projects are based on English lead sizes which are still in inches. Lead is made in various widths and hearts (see Diag. 3). The 'H' section kind can be flat or rounded, made by milling or extruding; the 'U' section and corner section lead is extruded (forced through a die under pressure); and there are many kinds of extruded leads for different purposes. The use of flat or rounded lead is a matter of preference; sometimes I use both kinds in the same panel to give variety to the texture of the glazing. Stained glass artists tend to use milled lead for large-scale commissions such as church windows: this lead has been forced between two wheels and, when once pulled taut, will retain its tension.

Further glazing requirements (see Fig.2)

Glazing board (2)
Beginners making small panels need not get a larger one than 610mm (2ft) square. Deal is the best wood, since it does not splinter no matter how many nails are put in it; but blockboard will do.

Laths (battens) (8)
These are thin strips of wood with which to make a right-angle on the glazing board so that the panel can be constructed square. For a 610mm (2ft) glazing board you need three strips 50mm (2in) wide × 457mm (18in) long × 10mm (⅜in) deep.

Glazing nails (1)
Nowadays we use horseshoe nails, replacing the old glazing nails. They are flat-sided and so do not chip the glass. These nails secure the glass pieces as they are built up in their leads before soldering. Twenty-four should be enough for small-scale panels.

Solder
This is sold by the strip or, more economically, by the kilo. The usual ratio of lead to tin is 60/40.

Flux (6)
You can use a paste (6a) or liquid (6b) applied with a brush (6c). Tallow candle (7) is traditionally used for lead work. This is a special wickless candle: do not use ordinary candle. Powdered resin can also be used.

Abrasive material (15) (16)
Materials such as wire wool grade 0/00 or file card (used for cleaning files and found in a good tool shop) are used to clean joints prior to soldering. A wire suede brush is also suitable. Do not use an ordinary wire brush: it is too fierce.

Putty
For large windows, stained glass artists use a liquid cement which can be bought ready mixed; but for small panels an ordinary putty (for wood or metal) can be used. Darken it by using a little grate polish (20), obtainable from hardware stores.

Scrub brush (19)
An old boot brush (bristles not too short) can be used to brush up the leads to give them a proper finish.

Tools

Glasscutter (10a, b) and cutting oil.
An ordinary steel single-wheel cutter can be bought at any hardware shop; tungsten-wheel cutters are also available. Such cutters are perfectly adequate for the beginner. Stained glass stockists also have on sale a Supercutter: this is a sophisticated tool with a built-in oil supply to keep the wheel permanently lubricated. It is easier to hold than the simple traditional cutter, but more costly. Buy a fine-grade machine oil for lubricating your cutter, or a cutting oil from your stained glass stockist.

Pliers (11) (12)
A pair of ordinary household pliers can be used, but the more specific the tool, the better it will do its job. Grozing pliers nibble away jagged edges or chew out particular shapes. Breaking pliers are for breaking long strips of glass. Cut-running pliers deal with long straight lines or gentle curves.

diag. 2 Key to Fig. 2, numbered:
1 Glazing nails 2 Glazing board
3 Soldering iron linked to a dimmer switch (3b) to control the current
4 Iron stand 5 Temperature-controlled iron 6a Paste flux
6b Liquid flux 6c Flux brush
7 Tallow candle 8 Laths 9 Flow pen
10a Single wheel glasscutter
10b Supercutter 11 Breaking pliers
12 Grozing pliers 13 Lead-cutting knife 14 Stopping knife 15 File card
16 Wire wool 17 Lathekin 18 Lead vice 19 Scrub brush 20 Grate polish
21 Pattern shears for cutting templates (see Chapter 2)

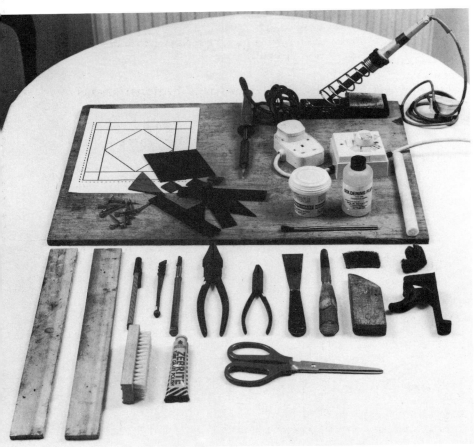

fig. 2 Tools for stained glass

Lead-cutting knife (13)
This chisel-shaped knife has a square end to its blade for cutting lead cleanly.

Stopping knife (14)
Stockists will have this converted oyster knife for lifting the leaf of the lead so that glass pieces can be put in position. Traditionally it was a dual-purpose tool with a weighted handle: this heavy end was used to tap in the glazing nails. Craftsmen now have to make their own; but you can use a hammer instead.

Lathekin (17)
A wedge-shaped wooden tool for opening up the heart (channel) of the lead.

Lead vice (18)
An ordinary vice can be made to work; otherwise buy a lead vice. Lead has to be stretched before it can be used, to remove kinks and make it taut. Although it is possible to stand on one end and pull, or to wedge it in a door-jamb (damaging the wood) and pull the other end, you will find that there is more luck than judgement involved in these methods!

Soldering iron (3a, b) (5)
There are two kinds of electric iron on the market. The cheaper ones have no temperature control (3a) so must be turned on and off regularly to prevent overheating. They can be controlled by attaching a dimmer switch system (3b) which controls the input of electricity. The thermostatically-controlled iron (5) is dearer, but it remains at a constant temperature and so there is no possibility of it burning your work. If you are going to make more than a little stained glass, you will find the simpler type frustrating. Don't buy too low-powered an iron: it must be 75 or 100 watt. Check the instructions to find out how to look after the tip of the iron of your particular model.

Soldering iron stand (4)
A stand of some kind is recommended, but the kind that has a place for a damp sponge on which to wipe the tip is very convenient.

Pattern shears (21)
These special scissors are needed if you are going to use the template method of cutting glass (see p. 62).

Grinder
This machine is very useful for cutting out shapes if you are going to make many stained glass items, especially in the copperfoil technique which requires perfect accuracy in cutting. However, I would advise everyone to learn to cut with a glasscutter first, as relying on a grinder could be a problem if it should break down. A grinder is illustrated in Fig. 31.

Safety hints

Wash your hands with soap and water after handling lead; if sensible precautions are taken, there can be no harm in using it.

Have a box of assorted plasters by you and, if you cut yourself, wash the area *immediately*, pat dry and cover with a plaster. A cut from glass is a clean cut, but carrying on working is not wise as dirt can then penetrate the cut.

Don't bring snacks near your work: grozings do not improve a cup of tea!

PROJECT 1: 'Greek Cross' beginner's panel
Basic level: 21 pieces

This pattern, a hanging panel for a window, with a simple cross design, consists of straight lines only. It has been designed for the beginner to learn the basics of colour-choosing, glasscutting and glazing. The cutline for the panel is 300mm (11⅘in) square, but the full size (including lead frame) is 305mm (12in) square.

Colour choosing

Diag. 5 shows four ways in which colour selection can interpret the design. Colour sense needs training, so

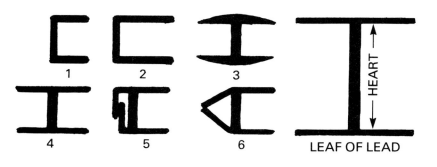

diag. 3 Different lead sections: 1 'C' lead; 2 'U' lead; 3 round lead; 4 flat lead; 5 flat lead folded to make 'U' shape; 6 flat lead pressed together to cover heart. 5 and 6 are suitable only for flat leads 9.5mm (⅜in) upwards.

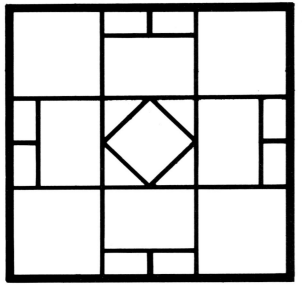

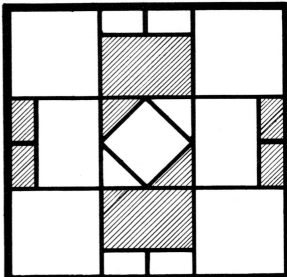

a

diag. 4 Project 1: 'Greek Cross' – reduced cartoon

you should build up a range of coloured glass samples and spend a little time, regularly, playing around to see how the colours affect one another. Take a sheet of plain glass and stick on pieces of coloured glass by putting a little plasticine all along their under edges. Put it on a window sill and stand back from it. Different colours influence each other, according to how they are juxtaposed. If you place a very dark tone among a number of light tones, it accentuates the contrast: you will see that the balance has been destroyed. Remember that, generally speaking, all 'warm' colours – reds, oranges, yellows – come forward; all 'cool' colours – blues, greens, greys – recede.

Copy the 'Greek Cross' design (Diag. 4) several times and colour it in different ways, noticing how the colour choice affects the way you 'read' the pattern. When you have decided on your final choice, stick to this colour design and don't change it at the last minute. Buy your coloured glass and other materials as specified.

Materials required

Glass

45 sq cm ($1\frac{1}{2}$ sq ft), which allows for wastage. With careful cutting, two standard cut-up sheets (sold as 203mm (8in) × 304mm (12in) by stockists) will suffice.

Lead

1 calm 9.5mm ($\frac{3}{8}$in) × 6.3mm ($\frac{1}{4}$in) heart or 4.7mm

c

diag. 5 Four ways of interpreting the design

($\frac{3}{16}$in) heart outside lead;
2 calms 6.3mm ($\frac{1}{4}$in) × 6.3mm ($\frac{1}{4}$in) × 4.7mm ($\frac{3}{16}$in) heart lead.

Solder
2 sticks.

The cutline

Enlarge Diag. 6 (cutline) to the size described below. In Chapter 2, p.26, are full details of how to enlarge a design to make a cartoon (working drawing), and from the cartoon you always make your cutline. However, to make things simple for Project 1, merely

b

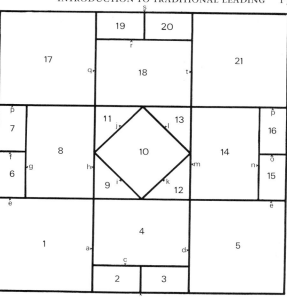

diag. 6 Project 1: reduced cutline with glazing sequence (enlarge to 300mm (11⅘in) square)

How to cut glass

Practising with plain glass
Practise on ordinary window glass. Off-cuts and scraps can often be obtained at little or no cost from your local glass merchant. Confidence is the key to successful glasscutting, so practise as much as possible. Time spent practising on plain glass at this stage will save you money and frustration when you come to cut your coloured glass. Cut on a flat surface covered with one layer of an old blanket. Have a dustpan and brush handy to brush up chippings frequently. Dispose of them carefully. Always wipe glass clean with a dry cloth before cutting.

How to hold a glasscutter (Diag. 7)
If using a traditional single-wheel cutter, place the ball of the thumb on the underneath of the handle and the index finger on the top: the shaft of the cutter rests in the fork of the first two fingers. The aim is to exert an even pressure on the wheel so that it scores the glass. There will be a tendency for your forefinger to bend, but do try to keep it straight, and persevere in the correct hold for this tool. If you have bought a Supercutter, it is cylindrical and held like a pen. It is much easier to use than the simple tool (and it oils its wheel automatically from its reservoir), but it is considerably dearer. The wheel of the simple cutter should be kept well oiled: have a little cap holding cotton wool soaked in oil and dip the wheel in

d

enlarge Diag. 6. On a piece of paper, draw with pencil the panel frame 300mm (11⅘in) square, checking the right-angles. Divide it into 100mm (3 15/16 in) squares. Plot all the shapes on the diagram. When you have pencilled in all the shapes accurately, go over them with a black felt-tip pen, making sure your pencil line is in the centre of the black line you are now making, which should be approximately 2mm (1/16 in) thick. This line represents the heart of the lead.

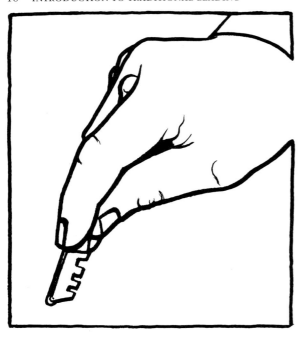

diag. 7 How to hold a glasscutter

frequently. The tip of the wheel cuts the glass, so hold the tool upright – not leaning to one side.

Cutting glass: straight lines

First practise cutting straight lines freehand, getting used to the tool and finding the right pressure. For straight lines you bring the cutter *towards* you; for curves and shapes you must push the glasscutter *away* from you, otherwise you cannot see the shape you are trying to cut out. Practise both procedures, scoring towards and away from you. Score the glass by drawing a line with the cutter from top to bottom of a piece of plain glass, keeping an even pressure. There should now be a thin silver line on the glass; and the sound should be a gentle hiss. When you score the glass there should not be a white line or any glass flakes: if this happens, you are exerting too much pressure, and will tire your hand. If the pressure has not been even, the silver line will disappear from time to time and the score cannot be considered successful. *Never go over the same score twice*: it will blunt the cutter and be no guarantee of getting your shape. Make another score line 13mm ($\frac{1}{2}$in) or so further over. When you have managed a continuous silver line, you may proceed to the next step.

Snapping the scored glass by hand

There are various ways of breaking glass along the score. For straight lines you can use snapping. To achieve a clean, even break, take the glass firmly in both hands, thumbs on top of the glass at an equal distance either side of the scored line. Exert an even pressure on either side of the score line and *bend down* and *pull apart* at the same time. This brisk action will result in a clean break. Do *not* hold one side and pull down on the other: you risk grazing your knuckles.

Blunting the edges

It is essential to get into the habit of dulling the edges *immediately* you have cut any glass. This is done by drawing the edges of the two pieces of glass at right angles to each other along their entire length. Blunt *both* edges on *both* pieces of glass. You can use a carborundum stone if you prefer. This dulling action must become an automatic procedure after cutting every piece of glass, as the edges are razor-sharp until dulled.

Tapping out straight lines

If you are unable to snap the glass, you may tap it out, but it does not give such a clean edge. Holding the glasscutter in the hand as if for glass scoring, turn your hand over and tap the glass underneath the score line with the metal head of the glasscutter, opposite the wheel end. If your glasscutter has a ball end, this is meant for tapping the glass. Tap with a firm yet relaxed action all along the underneath of the score line. You can see it cracking as you go. Don't keep tapping at the same place – go along the line, then repeat the action if it hasn't cracked. You must hold both pieces of glass as you tap, so that when you have tapped the piece out, it doesn't drop on the floor. Hold your work over the table with your blanket on it so that if you can't hold one piece as it is tapped out, it hasn't too far to fall. The edge will not be a clean cut so you will need to groze it.

Grozing: trimming the edges

The notches on your glasscutter are designed for grozing but I advise grozing pliers for greater accuracy. When using grozing pliers you must have control over the jaws, so hold them with the index finger between the handles and use this first finger to control the opening and closing of the jaws. You only need to exert sufficient pressure to take off the protruding pieces of glass to straighten the edge. You must not exert full pressure or you might crack the glass. Breaking pliers can also be used for snapping off small straight lines. Put the jaws of the pliers up to the score line half-way along its length (protect the glass from chipping by putting a piece of cloth between the jaws) and pull down. The glass will break neatly all along the score line.

Cut-running pliers

These special pliers, used for snapping straight edges, have a notch on the bottom jaw. When the score is aligned with the guide line on top of the pliers, and these are squeezed, it causes the crack to run along the score line, thus breaking the glass in a single action.

Cutting glass for a panel

I urge you to cut a few of the shapes out of plain glass, just for practice; then, when you feel confident, start on the coloured glass. Before starting to cut, wipe both sides clean. Choose the best side for cutting – this is always the smoothest side. Waterglass, for example, has a gently rippled surface, and so one must cut on the reverse.

There are two methods of cutting glass shapes: the free-cutting method (used in Great Britain and sometimes called the English Method) and the template method (used in Europe and in the USA). I was brought up on the free-cutting method. This way has the advantage of not having to bother with templates except when the glass is too dark to see through or when using opalescent glass. For the template method see p. 62.

An improvised light-table

If you cannot see the cutline through your glass because its tone is too dark or opaque, and you prefer not to get involved in making templates, you can see to cut your glass on an improvised light-table. With light shining through the cutline you will be able to see the outline to be cut. Rig up a light-table by using a sheet of thick glass (no less than 7mm ($\frac{1}{4}$in) plate), with bevelled or taped edges, balanced on wood blocks or bricks. The glass must be at least 229mm (9in) above the table to allow the heat of the light-bulb placed underneath to escape.

Free-cutting method

Don't rush in: lay your coloured sheets on your cutline and, referring to your coloured design, spend some time working out how you are going to get all your shapes out of the glass as economically as possible. Use a felt-tip pen to mark out the required shapes on your glass. If you have a straight edge or a right-angle already in your glass sheet, incorporate it into your piece. When cutting, lay the glass on the cutline *just inside* the black line – that represents the heart of the lead. For beginners, I recommend ruling the pieces in this project, using your lath as a guide. Later, you will be able to cut short straight pieces freehand. If you have bought large sheets of glass (larger than the hobbyist 204mm (8in) × 304mm (12in) cut size) work out the area you require by tracing the shapes from the cutline with a felt-tip pen. If you cut a small shape out of a

large sheet, you risk cracking it, so now cut off what you need from the main body of the glass. As you cut your shapes, mark each piece of glass and the cutline shape with the colour's initial and check it on the cutline.

Checking the glass on the cutline

When you have finished cutting all your pieces of glass, lay them on the cutline according to their colours. Check that each piece of glass is just within the black line which represents the heart of the lead. I cannot stress too strongly that you must check your glass carefully at this stage and groze it if necessary so that it fits perfectly. If you sort out any problems at this point, it will minimise problems at the glazing stage. Remove the pieces from the cutline in preparation for glazing.

Glazing

This term includes all the processes of assembling the panel: leading, soldering, puttying, and fixing hooks.

Stretching the ouside lead calms

All lead must be stretched to make it taut before it can be used. A calm of lead is normally stretched then 'dressed' before cutting. I would advise you to stretch the whole calm as it is less wasteful. A lead vice is the best tool for the job, but an ordinary vice will suffice. Place one end of the lead (9.5mm ($\frac{3}{8}$in) × 6.3mm ($\frac{1}{4}$in) or 4.8mm ($\frac{1}{16}$in) heart) in a vice so that it grips; take the other end in a pair of pliers and pull. Your right foot should be placed behind the left with legs slightly apart. Keep your weight on the left (front) foot and do not lean backwards! Pull with your arms to stretch the lead: pull steadily until it feels stiff. Do not on any account hold the pliers in front of your stomach, but to your right-hand side, in case the lead snaps.

Cutting the lead calm

If you are working in a limited space, it might be easier for you to cut the lead into strips now, before dressing it; although that is not the sequence in a studio. For ease of handling, you might like to cut four strips from your calm now which will form the frame of your panel. The amount you will need is four pieces of 300mm (11$\frac{4}{5}$in) *plus* an allowance, at this learning stage, for mistakes. I suggest another 50mm (2in); so cut four strips of 350mm (approx 14in).

To cut your lead, take a very sharp chisel-bladed knife (it must be kept very sharp with an oilstone); place this knife handle in the middle of your palm, put the blade squarely on the lead, holding the lead steady with the left hand, and exert a downward pressure on the knife with a gentle rocking motion. Keep the blade

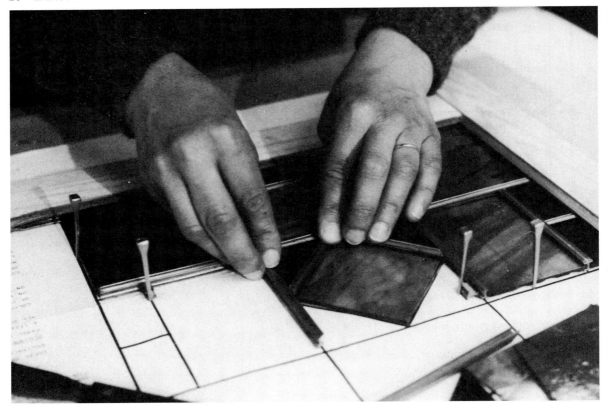

fig. 3 Assembling Project 1

vertical in order to cut square. Don't press too hard: you will squash the lead. Cut three more identical lengths.

Dressing the lead
Any kinks in the leaf of the lead must be removed. Lay a strip of lead on a smooth surface and take a stopping knife; run the blade along the bottom leaf of the lead which is nearest to you, pressing lightly down (not sideways) as you work from right to left. Then, working from left to right, go back along the lead dressing the bottom leaf, which is furthest from you. Remember, the lead is 'H' in section and can be said to have four leaves. Carefully roll the lead over and dress the other two leaves. You must aim at keeping your lead in perfect condition, as nothing gives a panel a worse appearance than mangled lead. Dress the other three strips.

Setting up the board
Take your glazing board and tape the cutline to it, allowing space for the laths. They must be placed at the bottom left-hand corner, thus forming a right angle.

Take one piece of dressed lead, lay it along the bottom outside line so that the heart of the lead corresponds to the black line of the cutline. Take a lath and place it up against the outside of the lead. *Lightly* nail the lath into position (it might need adjustment). Do the same with the second strip of outside lead so that you have formed a right angle. Check with a set square that your angle is 90°. Take glass piece *1* that goes into the bottom left-hand corner and slide it into the lead, first in the side then the bottom strip, checking that the glass is just inside the black line on the cutline. As you checked your glass after cutting it, you know it must be the right size. You must therefore adjust your laths a fraction if necessary; then nail them down firmly when you are satisfied that they are in the right position.

Mitring the outside leads
Your bottom lead is in its horizontal position along the bottom lath. Check that the end in the left-hand corner is square; recut (on lath or elsewhere on the board) if necessary. Take your left-hand vertical lead, make sure one end is square, and lay it along the vertical lath so that its (checked) end in the corner is lying directly on top of the end of the horizontal lead (Diag. 8a). Using a nail or lead knife, mark on the horizontal lead where

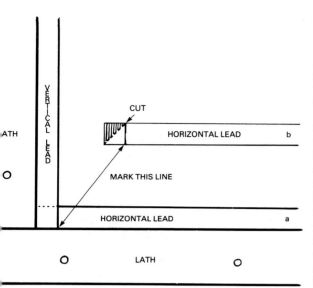

diag. 8 How to mitre the bottom left outside leads

the vertical lead is crossing it: now you have made a box shape at the end of the horizontal lead (Diag. 8b). You must now cut the mitre, but this must *never* be done in position on the cutline, as it would get cut to ribbons. Remove the lead and cut it on the lath or elsewhere on the board. To get your mitre, cut an exact

diag. 9 How to mitre the top left outside leads

diagonal, bottom left to top right of the box as shown on the diagram. The knife must be upright when cutting. Repeat the process at the end of the vertical lead and fit the two halves of the mitre into the left-hand corner. Secure the horizontal lead by putting a glazing nail at its right-hand end.

Now mitre the other end of the vertical lead. This must be done accurately: if you make a mistake you must cut a new strip of lead. Take glass piece *17* (top left-hand square), place it on the cutline inside the lead, checking it is inside the right-hand black line. Cut one 25mm (1in) gauge from your leftover piece of outside lead and place it on the top outside line, making sure that the glass square is inside the lead (Diag. 9a). Place your top horizontal outside lead over the gauge and the left-hand vertical lead; mark a box on the vertical lead which is underneath (Diag. 9b) (you will need to mark on either side of the top horizontal lead to make the box). Cut the mitre, top left-hand corner to bottom right-hand corner of the box. Repeat the process at the right-hand end of the bottom horizontal lead, glass piece *5*.

Each mitre must be cut separately: don't make one and copy it in case it is wrong. An alternative to the method outlined above is to use a mitre block.

Assembling the glass pieces
The order in which to do this is shown on the cutline: the glass pieces are numbered and the leading sequence indicated by lower-case letters. Work along the bottom line from left to right. Take glass piece *1* and place

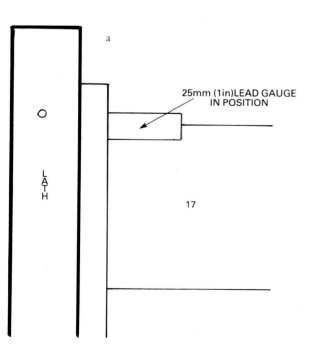

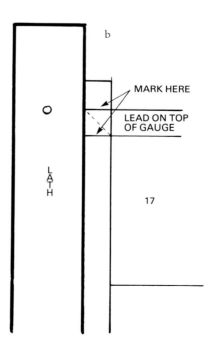

it in its leads. The glass should always be on or just inside the black line of the cutline. At the top of your glass piece *1*, tap two glazing nails, upright, with their flat sides to the glass, so they do not chip it. It is useful to place a scrap of lead between the glass and the nail to protect painted work; but it is essential to use these protectors once the lead is in position, or else the nail would damage the leaf of the lead. All this is clearly shown in Fig. 3.

Preparing the inside leads
Take your calm of inside lead, 6.3mm ($\frac{1}{4}$in) × $\frac{1}{4}$in × 4.8mm ($\frac{3}{16}$in) heart and stretch it. Depending on the manufacturer, it could be somewhat longer than the outside lead calm. I advise you to cut the calm in half for ease of handling. Dress the two halves. Cut off two little pieces of lead, 13mm ($\frac{1}{2}$in) long, to act as gauges. Then cut all your lead strips for the panel: (the lengths allow for mistakes in trimming) two at 318mm (12$\frac{1}{2}$in); 10 at 114mm (4$\frac{1}{2}$in); four at 89mm (3$\frac{1}{2}$in) and four at 38mm (1$\frac{1}{2}$in).

Commencing glazing
Place lead *a* in position to the right of *1*, It will need trimming. Do this following Diag. 11. Your lead gauge will show you where to make a mark on lead *a* in order to trim. Place the gauge along the top of *1* butted up against the upright lead *a*, making sure that the glass is properly in the lead; it should touch the heart. Mark a line continuing the line of the gauge: this is where you must trim your lead. Remove it, trim, then put it back in place (Diag.11).

Next, place *2* in position, hold with a glazing nail and place in lead *b*. Trim according to method shown

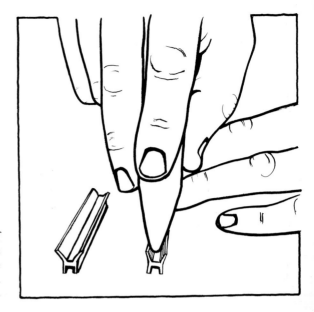

diag. 10 Using a lathekin

in Diag. 11. Continue to glaze pieces *3, 4* and *5*, following the cutline sequence. Don't forget to place two glazing nails to the right of *5*. Now take the long lead *e* and put it into position, taking out the glazing nails and securing the bottom row of glass pieces as you fit. It will need trimming at the right-hand end. Use the outside lead gauge and place it on the outside line just below where the *e* lead comes across. Mark off and trim. Continue glazing pieces *6, 7* and *8*.

Use of lathekin (Diag. 10)
If for any reason the glass does not fit into the lead easily, you need to open it. This is done with the lathekin: insert the pointed end of the tool into the lead and run down the length, lightly pressing on the heart.

Should you at any time find that your glass pieces are beginning to overlap the black line on the cutline, *don't* rush in and trim them. Find out what is causing the overlap. Take the glazing apart and discover the exact trouble spot. Often it is caused by not putting the glass into the lead properly. As your panel builds up, if it is a fraction full, you can gently tap your glass into place with the weighted end of a stopping knife or a hammer and wood block. The glazing must not be too tight, otherwise the glass will crack under the pressure. The aim of glazing is to suspend the glass pieces in the mesh of the lead.

Glazing the central diamond-pane section
The trickiest part of the glazing comes in the fitting of lead *i* and *9* through to *l* and *13* because you have got to

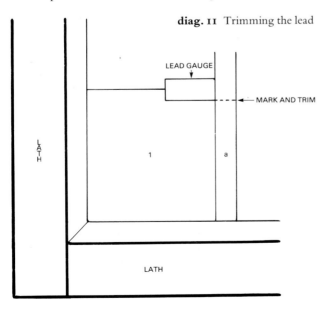

diag. 11 Trimming the lead

LEAD GAUGE

MARK AND TRIM

LATH

1

a

LATH

cut the correct angles to the leads so that they fit properly at the points of the diamond shape. Take lead *i* and, following Diag. 12, place it diagonally along piece *9*. Take your two lead gauges (inside lead) and place them as shown: mark where to cut, then trim at both ends. Place *9* in position, fit lead *i*; put *10* in position, trim lead *j*; and so on till the central area is glazed.

Glazing the rest of the panel

Pieces *14–21* are glazed on the same principles as explained in glazing *1–8*. Complete the glazing including the insertion of *21*.

Completing the panel's outside leads

Mark and cut the mitre on one end of each of the remaining outside lead strips. Fit the right-hand outside lead, checking that the right-hand bottom corner mitre fits properly. Do this by removing the glazing nails *two at a time*, slipping in the mitred end of lead and securing it in position by a glazing nail, not forgetting the scrap of lead in between the lead and the nail to prevent any damage to the leaf.

Your right-hand vertical lead will now be securely in position. Mark the mitre angle on this lead according to the method in Diag. 8b; remove the lead, securing the right-hand side of the panel with glazing nails, cut the mitre and *put to one side* (you can't put it back in position as it will be in the way of measuring the mitre on the top lead). Take your top piece of outside lead, carefully remove the glazing nails, two at a time, and fit, checking the mitre at the top left-hand corner. Then mark your mitre at the right-hand end, and remove the lead, not forgetting to secure the panel with glazing nails; cut and replace.

Final checking of the outside leads

Remove glazing nails along right-hand side of the panel and place a lath up against the lead. You must check that the right-hand corner is a true right-angle, and that the outside lead is perfectly straight. If it is not, gently tap the side of the lath with a stopping knife handle until it is square. If the outside lead is still irregular, put the stopping knife blade under the leaf of the lead keeping the lath steady, and press firmly: this will eliminate any unevenness. Remove the lath and renail, not forgetting the use of protectors. Repeat the process with the top lead; then nail the lath into position, putting nails in on the far side of the lath. You must train yourself to perfect accuracy at this stage. This particular panel is to hang in a window; but in the future you might like to make a panel for a given aperture, and any sloppy glazing will result in the panel not fitting its opening. Your panel is now ready for soldering.

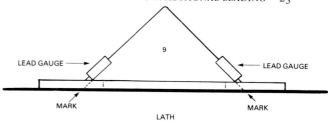

diag. 12 Cutting the leads on the central diamond motif

Soldering the panel

Lead oxidises so you must clean your leads. A fine wire brush as used for suede, wire wool grade 0/00, or a file card are all suitable for cleaning. Carefully rub all the joins you intend to solder immediately. If you have to leave your work for a day or more, then you will need to clean your joins again. A flux must be used to make the solder run. Various types are available, the most convenient being paste and liquid flux (both applied with a flux brush), and tallow candle (lay the end onto the join and give the candle a little twist, depositing a small amount). (See Health & Safety, page 116.)

Place a little flux on the join, take your stick of solder in your (left) hand and put it on the join; then lay the tip of your hot iron on top of the solder and allow it to melt properly. *Don't* move the tip of the iron about. Students tend to think they should spread the solder; but moving the iron tip merely prevents it melting the solder properly. Just lift off the iron and you will find you have a smooth join. Fig. 5 illustrates good and bad solder joins. There are three satisfactory joins on the first lead coming from the left-hand outside lead: these are doing their job of joining the leads and contributing to the good appearance of the finished panel. Above this lead, and a little to the right, are three badly soldered joins. The first shows what happens if you forget to flux the join: the solder won't run; the second (to the right) has been done with an iron which is not hot enough: the solder has come up in an ugly and dangerous point; the third (top, on outside lead) has been spoilt because the iron was too hot: the solder just melts away.

If your iron is not thermostatically-controlled, you must take great care not to let your iron overheat and melt not only the solder but the lead too. This type of iron must be turned off frequently to prevent it overheating. I advise you to test-solder two scraps of lead whenever you know your iron is reaching its maximum safety temperature, and turn it off for a few minutes if you see the lead melting. In fact it might be a useful warning to let the lead actually melt, so that you realise the damage a too-hot iron can do. An ordinary

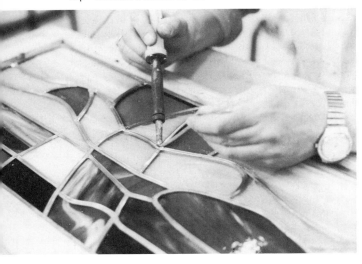

fig. 4 Soldering

iron can be controlled by fixing a dimmer switch between it and the electricity source as shown in Fig. 2, item 3b.

A proper bench-holder is very useful to place your iron in when not in use, and it has a compartment for a damp sponge on which you must wipe the iron tip frequently, to keep its silver tip clean: it will not work if it gets black.

Work systematically on soldering all the joins, starting at the top. Be sure you do not miss a join.

Turning the panel
Never pick up a panel as if it were a tray: it is not rigid, and, especially with larger-scale work, will sag and possibly crack. Remove all nails and laths. Slide the panel to the edge of the bench so that it overhangs by about half its length; keeping it supported by your left hand, allow it to drop, the bench edge still taking its weight. Then quickly bring it to an upright position and stand it on its edge on the bench. Turn it round and repeat the action in reverse to place it back on the bench. Clean and solder every join on the back of the panel.

Attaching the hooks (Diag. 13)
I have recommended you to use H section outside lead, as it is easy to fit neat hooks in it. It is possible to use U section lead, but then there is a problem in fitting neat hooks; my method is for H section lead. Take a piece of copper wire about 152mm (6in) long, stretch it in a vice to make it taut, and bend it into a narrow U shape using a nail around which to form a curve. Take your pliers and squeeze the head of the U shape so that the whole hook comes together, having a spring in it. Clean and flux the inside of your lead frame at the top right-hand corner. Fix the hook inside the exposed leaf

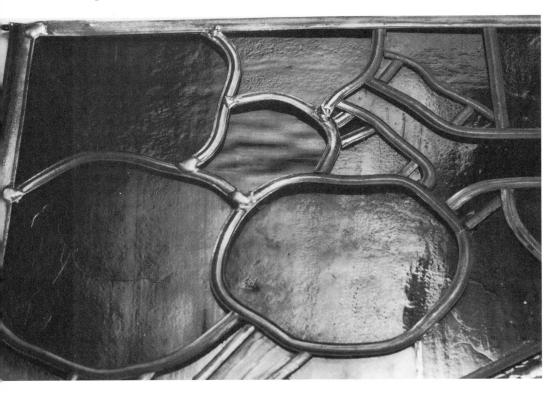

fig. 5 Good and bad solder joins

of the H section, the curved head at the top, protruding just a fraction. This can be seen in Fig. 5 demonstrating solder joins: remember that the top of the panel is on the left-hand side of this photograph. Solder into position. Form and fix the second hook.

Puttying the panel

Turn the panel on its front. It now needs to be made rigid. Some people think that a little panel need not be puttied, but I consider it essential, not only to give it a firm feel, but to prevent light seeping around the leads and dulling the colour effect. Also, if you are using hand-made glass, which is uneven in thickness, the putty will fill in the space between the lead and the glass. Of course the main reason for puttying/cementing a panel, which traditionally went in an actual window aperture, was to weatherproof it. A type of liquid cement is used in large-scale windows, but is not economical for little panels. Buy a metal/wood glazing putty and add a little grate polish to blacken it. Carefully push the putty under the leaf of all the leads, using a blunt knife or your thumb. If you need to lift the leaf of any of the leads with your stopping knife in order to put the putty in, gently press the leads down afterwards.

Cleaning the panel

Sharpen a wooden stick the size of a pencil and clean up the excess putty by running the point round the edges of the leads. This must be done *immediately* after puttying. Then brush the panel with a scrub brush. Turn the panel over and putty the other side: this will not take so much putty. Clean it up and brush it. Turn the panel onto its front again and clean up any seepage from the back.

Blackening the leads

I often see small panels with their leads left silver. This was never the custom in the stained glass studios: they always blackened the leads because they knew that it helped to bring out the full richness of the colour in the glass. It will also help camouflage any unevenness in your soldering! Put a tiny amount of blacking onto your scrub (boot) brush and brush the entire panel vigorously until the leads start to turn black. Continue to brush until all the blacking has come off the glass. Treat the back in the same way. Don't worry if a slight smear of oils from the putty is over the glass. Leave the putty to harden over two to three days, then take a soft brush and burnish it all over: the leads will come up like ebony. There is no need to wipe each pane with a cloth or wash the panel. Whenever you want to clean it, brush with a soft brush.

Hanging the panel

Hang your panel in a good light and remember that our northern climate with its fitful sunshine, cloud banks and showers is ideal for stained glass. Your panel will have as many moods as the weather and you will not tire of looking at it.

Storing materials

Storing glass

This book aims to show you how you can use every scrap of glass in a wide variety of techniques, so that you never have to waste any of what has become, through rising energy costs, an almost semi-precious material. However, to use it efficiently you need to store it systematically. A simple rack can house all the larger pieces, standing end on. As your stock grows, you should store the pieces according to type, in their colour ranges. It is important to remember the type of glass to which each piece belongs, because if you wish to do a fused project, the glasses must all be of the same type. All the scraps should be sorted into types and colours and kept in trays: gardening or photographic trays are useful and inexpensive. Fragments should be put in jars: even the tiniest pieces can be used in appliqué and fused glass techniques.

Storing lead

Ideally, unstretched calms should be kept in a long lead box in a horizontal position. Maybe you can find a place under a piece of furniture where they can be laid out where they will not get knocked. Only stretch the amount of lead you need to use, and, once stretched, treat it with great care, as the good appearance of your finished panel depends on the condition of your lead. Any stretched lead which is over *must* be kept flat. However, since most people are short of space, it is acceptable to roll the lead calm into a loose coil to store it compactly. When you need to stretch it, carefully unroll it on a table, making sure it does not get twisted.

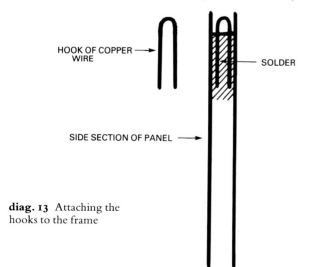

HOOK OF COPPER WIRE →

← SOLDER

SIDE SECTION OF PANEL →

diag. 13 Attaching the hooks to the frame

CHAPTER TWO

Graded projects
in traditional leading

In Chapter 1 you learnt all the basic steps in glazing a simple panel. I now assume that you have grasped these techniques and are ready to proceed to more difficult projects. The following five panels are graded in order of difficulty, each one intended to develop aspects of traditional glazing skills (Project 6 can also be made as a copperfoil wall plaque). The increasing complexity of the designs will challenge your colour sense, give you a chance to experiment with different types of glass and understand the use of various widths of lead. Working through these projects will enable you to design more successfully for the medium, because you will know what the practical demands of stained glass are.

TECHNIQUES

Enlarging the cartoon

Projects 2 to 6 are each illustrated by a miniature cartoon which you must enlarge to the size you prefer. I have indicated the size I envisage for the panel. Photocopying shops, especially those specialising in architectural services, have machines which will enlarge to your requirements, but if you prefer to enlarge the cartoon yourself, this can be done by drawing a grid on tracing paper over the miniature cartoon, then making a similar grid, proportionately larger, on paper and plotting the shapes on it. If you have to enlarge a complicated design, you will need a finer grid scheme to plot all the details accurately. All the lead widths must be blacked in on the cartoon so that you will have a clear idea of the effect of the finished panel. A cutline is made from the cartoon.

Making the cutline

Place strong tracing paper over the cartoon, fix it into position and draw down the centre of each lead line with a pencil. When you are sure you have done this carefully and checked that your right-angles are correct, remove the cartoon, take a black flow pen and ink in all the lines with a line 2mm ($\frac{1}{16}$in) thick. This line represents the heart of the lead.

Cutting curves and circles

Project 2 contains gentle curves; Project 4 gives you practice in cutting the full range of shapes, including near-circles; Project 5 has more awkward shapes, such as pieces 2 and 54. The principle of cutting gentle curves is no different from cutting straight lines: keep a steady pressure on the cutter but *push away* from you. Diag. 14a shows the steps in cutting a deep in-swinging curve: this concave shape is approached in stages. Diag. 14b illustrates how to cut circular shapes, again by doing it in stages. Plenty of practice with plain white glass will give you the confidence to cut the more difficult shapes. The tapping-out and grozing procedures detailed in Chapter 1 are applicable to the cutting of curves and awkward shapes as well as straight lines.

PROJECT 2: 'Windmill' panel
Basic level: 32 pieces

Requirements

The panel will be 305mm (12in) square including the outside leads (full size).

Glass
525 sq mm ($1\frac{3}{4}$ sq ft) allowing for wastage. With careful cutting, using three colours, three sheets of the standard 203mm (8in) × 305mm (12in) will suffice.

Lead

2 calms 6.3mm ($\frac{1}{4}$in) flat × 4.7mm ($\frac{3}{16}$in) heart; 1 calm
1.5mm ($\frac{3}{8}$in) × 4.7mm ($\frac{3}{16}$in) heart outside lead.

Solder

2 sticks.

This project teaches you how to cut gentle curves;
and the handling of a variety of lead lengths.

Steps in making the panel

1 Enlarge the reduced cartoon (Diag. 15).
2 Make the cutline.
3 Work out several colour schemes before deciding on
your glass.
4 Cut the glass.
5 Set up the board and glaze according to the sequence
shown in Diag. 15, and the following instructions:

Section 1

Fix laths and lay mitred outside leads in position,
forming a right-angle in the left-hand bottom corner.
Place glass piece *1* in position with five glazing nails.
Cut a length of stretched and dressed lead a little longer
than *a*, line it up with the edge of the glass and gently
mould the lead to the shape of the glass with its end just
over the outside lead. You can now see the angle at
which to cut *a* before inserting it. Trim it (remember to
remove it); fit lead *a* into place. Mark where it is to be

diag. 15 Project 2: 'Windmill' – reduced cartoon with
glazing sequence (the black dots indicate the position of the
glazing nails)

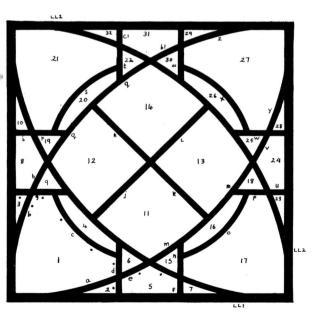

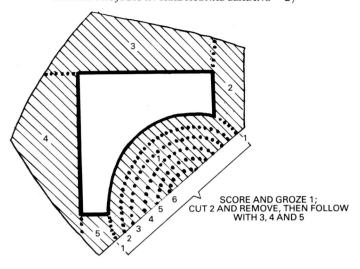

SCORE AND GROZE 1;
CUT 2 AND REMOVE, THEN FOLLOW
WITH 3, 4 AND 5

diag. 14a Cutting curves in easy stages
diag. 14b Cutting near-circular shapes in easy stages
(Project 4)

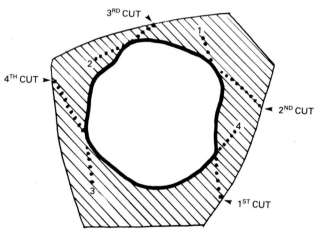

3RD CUT

4TH CUT

2ND CUT

1ST CUT

trimmed at the right-hand end; trim, fit into position
and insert glass piece *2*; secure with nail. I shall not
mention the insertion of nails again (see Diag. 15 for
their fixing points). Remove nails as you build up the
glazing pattern. Proceed according to the glazing
sequence until you have all glass pieces and leads in
place up to piece 10. You will now have an entire
section completed and held with nails all along the
curve. These will be moved two at a time when you fit
LL1.

Section 2

Take a length of lead a little longer than *LL1*; gently
press it into its curve along the cutline and mark off the
angle at one end. Mark the other end, cut and fit. Nail

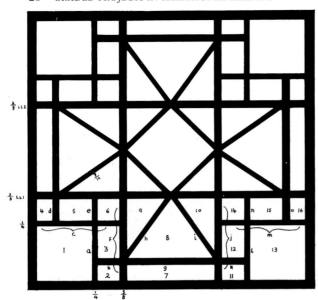

diag. 16 Project 3: 'Complex Cross' – reduced cartoon with glazing sequence

into position using scrap lead protectors except where glass piece *11* is to go. Glaze central area *11–14*.

Section 3
Glaze lower right-hand section, noting the sequence. Take care when sliding *17* into position.

Section 4
Glaze top left-hand section *19–22*. Fit *LL2*.

Section 5
Build up from piece *23*. Note that you will have a series of glazing nails along the right-hand outside lead line. From piece *27* onwards you will have a line of glazing nails along the top outside lead line too. When you come to fix the outside lead, remove glazing nails about two at a time and fit lead. On *no* account remove all the nails in one go as you run the risk of displacing all your pieces. The panel is now ready to solder.

PROJECT 3: 'Complex Cross' panel
45 pieces

Requirements

The panel will be 305mm (12in) square (full size, including the lead frame).

Glass
450 sq mm (1½ sq ft), allowing for wastage.

Lead
1 calm 12.7mm ($\frac{1}{2}$in) × 6.3mm ($\frac{1}{4}$in) or 4.7mm ($\frac{3}{16}$in) heart outside lead;
1 calm 9.5mm ($\frac{3}{8}$in) × 6.3mm ($\frac{1}{4}$in) or 4.7mm ($\frac{3}{16}$in) heart;
1 calm 6.3mm ($\frac{1}{4}$in) × 6.3mm ($\frac{1}{4}$in) or 4.7mm ($\frac{3}{16}$in) heart;
1 calm 4.7mm ($\frac{3}{16}$in) × 6.3mm ($\frac{1}{4}$in) or 4.7mm ($\frac{3}{16}$in) heart.

Solder
2 sticks.

This panel gives you a chance to exploit the optical effects possible with warm and cool colours, and to appreciate the refinement of using four different widths of lead.

Steps in making the panel

1 Enlarge the miniature cartoon (Diag. 16).
2 Make the cutline.
3 Work out several colour schemes before deciding on your glass. I suggest two possibilities:
 a Exploitation of advancing warm colours and receding cool colours. If you choose a red for the four triangles pointing to the central diamond, they will have a dramatic impact if set against a blue. Remember to balance the colours: the tonal strength of warm areas should be complemented by the same tonal range in the cool sections.
 b Contrasts achieved by white textured glasses, such as waterglass, reeded, glue chip, seedy and so on.
4 Cut your glass.
5 Set up the board and glaze according to the sequence shown on Diag. 16 and the following instructions:
 Note the use of the different lead widths, indicated in Diag. 24. Start in the left-hand corner and work across in three bands. Band one consists of pieces *1–16*. Take care to cut the leads accurately where they come to a point on the triangle and diamond shapes.

PROJECT 4: 'The Country Lane' panel
35 pieces

Requirements

The panel will be 305mm (12in) high × 324mm (12¾in) wide, full size.

Glass
525 sq mm (1¾ sq ft), allowing for wastage.

Lead
1 calm 12.7mm ($\frac{1}{2}$in) × 6.3mm ($\frac{1}{4}$in) or 4.7mm ($\frac{3}{16}$in)
heart outside lead;
1 calm 6.3mm ($\frac{1}{4}$in) × 6.3mm ($\frac{1}{4}$in) or 4.7mm ($\frac{3}{16}$in)
heart lead;
1 calm 4.7mm ($\frac{3}{16}$in) × 6.3mm ($\frac{1}{4}$in) or 4.7mm ($\frac{3}{16}$in)
heart lead.

Solder
2 sticks.

This panel contains a variety of shapes, including near-circular pieces, so that you can practise the full range of cutting and glazing. If you wish to paint this panel, full instructions and two illustrations can be found in Chapter 3.

Steps in making the panel

1 Enlarge the cartoon (Diag. 26) and make the cutline (Diag. 17).
2 Work out several colour schemes before selecting your glass. I suggest two possibilities:
  a *Naturalistic.* Foreground, middle ground and background in shades of green to blue. Tree: coloured according to your idea of the season. Sun and rays: golds. Sky: tints of blue. Road: brown. My panel (Fig. 16) uses English streaky rolled cathedral glass. I have chosen certain streaky patterns and strata in the glass to enhance the effect of movement on the ground and in the foliage, and cloud formations in the sky. These streaks in the glass suggest the way the glass should be painted. Note that the sunrays are made of waterglass which has a gently rippled surface and catches the light.
  b *Stylised*, using tones of one colour.
3 Cut your glass.

fig. 6 'The Country Lane': glazed back of panel. The top lead is in the process of being pressed together for a better appearance, as illustrated in Diag. 3, example 6

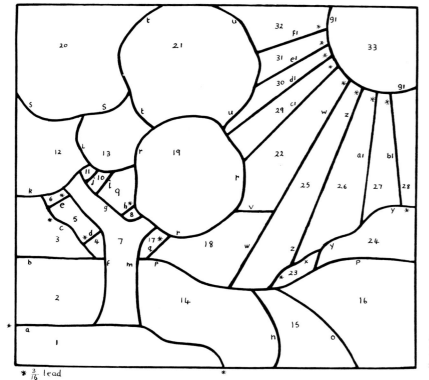

diag. 17 Project 4: 'The Country Lane' – reduced cutline with glazing sequence

4 Paint and fire your glass – see Chapter 3.

5 Glaze according to the sequence indicated on the cutline (Diag. 17). The different widths of lead can be seen in Fig. 6, and the narrow lead, 4.7mm ($\frac{3}{16}$in), is asterisked on Diag. 17.

Section 1 (pieces 1–13)

Note that *f* is a long lead (6.3mm [$\frac{1}{4}$in]) running along the left of the tree trunk.

Section 2 (pieces 14–21)

Long lead *p* gives definition to the horizon. Lead *r* is wrapped round piece *19*; the join must come at one of the intersections. Fig. 6, showing the back of the unfinished soldering, illustrates the neat join of lead *r* at the intersection with lead *q*.

Section 3 (pieces 22–33)

Note that *w* is a long 4.7mm ($\frac{3}{16}$in) lead. Pay attention to the sequence *23, 24, 25*. The sun disc, *g1*, is a 6.3mm ($\frac{1}{4}$in) lead.

PROJECT 5: 'Wheatears' panel

55 pieces

Requirements

This will measure 470mm ($18\frac{1}{2}$in) high × 190mm ($7\frac{1}{2}$in) wide, full size.

Glass

450sqmm ($1\frac{1}{2}$sqft), allowing for wastage.

Lead

1 calm 12.7mm ($\frac{1}{2}$in) × 6.3mm ($\frac{1}{4}$in) or 4.7mm ($\frac{3}{16}$in) heart outside lead;

2 calms 6.3mm ($\frac{1}{4}$in) × 6.3mm ($\frac{1}{4}$in) or 4.7mm ($\frac{3}{16}$in) heart.

Solder

2 sticks.

This stylised design develops dexterity in cutting and glazing the many small pieces and handling the variety of lead lengths.

Steps in making the panel

1 Enlarge the reduced cartoon to the size you require (Diag. 18).

2 Make the cutline.

3 Work out several colour schemes before deciding on the glass you require. I suggest three interpretations:

    a *Naturalistic.* Wheatears: golden streaky rolled cathedral glass; leaves: green streaky rolled cathedral

diag. 18 Project 5: 'Wheatears' – reduced cartoon with glazing sequence. A possible interpretation using glasspainting (tracing) is illustrated in the left-hand ear of corn.

glass; background: shades of blue waterglass. This interpretation would benefit from glasspainting (for instructions see Chapter 3).

b *Imaginative.* Wheatears: light brown one side, darker tone the other side. Tones of blue and green leaves; background of light-toned wispy glass.

c *Abstract.* Several different colours in the wheatears; red leaves; textured glass background.

4 Cut your glass. The second wheatear is *not* a mirror image, so you cannot cut two of everything: all pieces must be cut individually.

5 Glaze your panel following the sequence on the reduced cartoon (Diag. 18) and the following instructions:

Section 1 (pieces 1–16)
The rhythm of this section is created by the long leads *d* (from bottom of *2* to top of *4*), *g* (from bottom of *5* to top) and the lead which runs from the top to the bottom of the panel, called *LL1*. Be careful that the wheatear pieces fit properly just inside the cutline. Nail *LL1* with scrap protectors and check that every piece is in its correct position before proceeding to Section 2.

Section 2 (pieces 17–30)
Note that *x* is a long, flowing lead, from below *17* to the top, but *y* and *b1* are short, linking leads. Piece *26* must be put in position with accuracy before *27* and *28* can be fitted.

Section 3 (pieces 31–55)
Although the glass pieces are not a mirror image of the first wheatear, the glazing principles are the same. Lead *c1* runs from the top of *31* to the bottom of the panel. *LL2* which runs the whole length of the panel must be exactly in position or else it will spoil the glazing of the rest of the panel. Lead *t1* runs from the bottom of the panel to the side of piece *52*; *w1* springs from the border, between *51* and *52* and ends at *LL2* at the point of *54*.

PROJECT 6: 'Waterlily' panel
Very advanced: 80 pieces (copperfoil version pp. 80–1)

Requirements

This panel will measure $394\,\mathrm{sq\,mm}$ $(15\frac{1}{2}\,\mathrm{sq\,in})$, full size.

Glass
The curved shapes of the leaves and petals make for wastage, so allow $750\,\mathrm{sq\,mm}$ $(2\frac{1}{2}\,\mathrm{sq\,ft})$.

Lead
2 calms $12.7\,\mathrm{mm}$ $(\frac{1}{2}\mathrm{in}) \times 6.3\,\mathrm{mm}$ $(\frac{1}{4}\mathrm{in})$ or $4.7\,\mathrm{mm}$ $(\frac{3}{16}\mathrm{in})$ heart outside lead (frame);
1 calm $7.9\,\mathrm{mm}$ $(\frac{5}{16}\mathrm{in}) \times 6.3\,\mathrm{mm}$ $(\frac{1}{4}\mathrm{in})$ or $4.7\,\mathrm{mm}$ $(\frac{3}{16}\mathrm{in})$ heart (edges of lily pads);
1 calm $6.3\,\mathrm{mm}$ $(\frac{1}{4}\mathrm{in}) \times 6.3\,\mathrm{mm}$ $(\frac{1}{4}\mathrm{in})$ or $4.7\,\mathrm{mm}$ $(\frac{3}{16}\mathrm{in})$ heart (outer petals and background);

diag. 19 Project 6: 'Waterlily' – reduced cartoon with glazing sequence

2 calms 4.7mm ($\frac{3}{16}$in) × 6.3mm ($\frac{1}{4}$in) or 4.7mm ($\frac{3}{16}$in) heart (inner petals, centre, and veins of pads).

Solder
2 sticks.

This is a very advanced piece. As you are going to invest much time and skill in making it, I recommend the finest 'antique' hand-made glass. Note that the turnover of the lily pads should be in a contrasting glass (see colour plate 6). Pieces *12, 26* and *35* are meant to be water, as well as all the large pieces round the flower and pads. Design your own flower centre, using 4.7mm ($\frac{3}{16}$in) lead, or the more delicate copperfoil technique, see p.63. Glaze according to sequence on Diag. 19 and the following instructions:

Steps in making the panel

Section 1 (pieces 1–29)
Lead *b* is a 7.9mm ($\frac{5}{16}$in) strip which runs round the pad from *6* to *13*. Trim carefully where it runs along the frame, and keep its flowing line. Leaf *f* is a long central vein of the pad, from *12* to *7*; *k* is a short lead. Strip *l* (7.9mm [$\frac{5}{16}$in]) flows right round the lily pad and must be carefully trimmed where it runs along the frame. Note that *m* is a 6.3mm ($\frac{1}{4}$in) lead; *q* is a 4.7mm ($\frac{3}{16}$in) vein. Piece *19* is a small leaf area; *20* is also pad. Strip *r* is the central vein from *20* to *m*; *w* is a short lead. Don't miss out the tiny lead *x* between the pad and the frame above *28*. Then fit *29* and nail only.

Section 2 (pieces 30–41)
Cut lead *y* (7.9mm [$\frac{5}{16}$in]) carefully as it touches the frame: keep the line flowing. Note that *z* is a 6.3mm ($\frac{1}{4}$in): trim it carefully where it butts up against the frame. Try to keep the flow of line till *q2* round pieces *36* and *37*. Strip *d1* is a long 4.7mm ($\frac{3}{16}$in) central vein. Pay attention to the short *e1* and when you come to putty the panel, don't clean the putty right out of this curve: it will help to give it a graceful shape. Strip *j1* is a short 6.3mm ($\frac{1}{4}$in) lead. Nail *41* into position without its lead; put it in later.

Section 3 (pieces 42–72: the flower)
The leads for all the petals, e.g. the two parts of *k1*, need to be mitred for the best effect, except where advised otherwise (*48*). This will guarantee the graceful and rhythmic pattern of the petals. Take care that you are keeping within the cutline as you glaze the flower or when you come to *61* onwards, you will have trouble. Carefully trim one side of *n1* where it touches *19*. Make your flower centre and treat it as one piece. It must be inserted after petal *53*, otherwise it will be too difficult

to fit into position. The lead which surrounds it, *w1*, must join at an intersection, for neatness. Leads *f2* can butt up: a mitre is not suitable.

Section 4 (pieces 73–80)
These two areas are simple. Note that *q2* is a 7.9mm ($\frac{5}{16}$in) lead: trim so that it picks up from lead *y*.

DESIGNING YOUR OWN PANEL

I hope that if you have made the beginner's panel in Chapter 1 and at least two panels in this chapter, you will feel confident about designing your own panel.

Making a colour design to scale

From years of teaching students, the majority of whom have no design experience, I can say that the commonest fault is people being full of enthusiasm and magnificent visions, but impatient of the practical problems of actually *making* their panels. Stained glass is a strict discipline and you must be willing to start at the beginning and accept that the demands of the medium cannot be separated from the process of making a suitable design. Make a series of small designs with a pencil or flowpen, doodling freely, but concentrating on simple shapes. From the outset I advise you to work in scale: draw your sketches in a frame, rectangle, square or circle, whatever shape you want your panel to be, in a size which is simple to scale up

diag. 20 Simple illustration showing the positive/negative aspects of a design

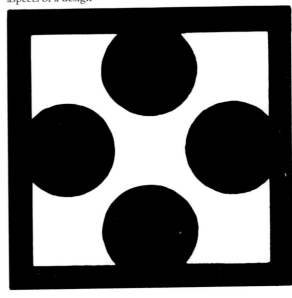

Glazed vestibule doors, private house, Hampstead, London (relates to Chapter 2)

'The Knight'—private collection, Albuquerque, New Mexico, USA (relates to Chapter 4)

3 'Elgar the Enigma'—artist's collection (relates to Chapter 4)

into your cartoon. Lay tracing paper over your rudimentary design and trace through the basic shapes; then lay another piece over that and modify/develop your ideas. This avoids the inhibiting act of rubbing out: your design must evolve with vitality and keep its spontaneity.

Remember that you will have to cut the shapes you have designed, so don't give yourself too much of a headache (or the expense of spoiling several pieces of glass). If you have a grinder, this machine will cut out very awkward shapes; but this is not a reason for designing difficult shapes, and the finest stained glass has always exhibited a striking simplicity. It is like an effective advertisement: the less complicated and cluttered the appearance, the more its message comes across. Also bear in mind that if you are designing for a panel more than 610mm (2ft) square, or a long panel, say 915mm (3ft) long by 305mm (1ft), you must take the strengthening requirements into consideration right from the design stage (see p.34).

Train yourself to think in shape and colour simultaneously; and *both* the shape and its background must be considered positively. Diag. 20 illustrates this point: this consists of a square with four black circles; refocus your eyes to look at the white areas and you will perceive a cross running diagonally. Learn to consider your designs in this way, assessing both the subject and its background as two interrelating halves. Beginners in stained glass design tend not to view the background positively: they put shapes against a 'dead' space; but in stained glass every area must 'read' definitely. When glass is considered too pictorially, instead of decoratively, we get an interesting shape against a mere void. Remember that the medium exploits a decorative mesh of lead lines within the confines of a panel or window. Every line and shape matters.

Another major factor in stained glass design is the effect of halation – the way that light erodes the lead and painted lines as it shines through the glass. The black leads are not merely structural, but play their part in controlling the light and helping the colours to be effective. Black is an integral part of your design. When you are satisfied with a design, work out the colour values and think through all the technical aspects before going any further. Although you may be itching to get on, I cannot emphasise too strongly that you cannot alter your design at a later stage, without cost and loss of time, so don't be tempted to gloss over technical matters thinking that you can adjust problems as you go along. Make your colour design to scale than draw the cartoon, on which the cutline is based (see p.26).

fig. 7 'The Radcliffe Camera': a light-box in a domestic setting

MAKING A LIGHT-BOX

A light-box is an underused method of displaying stained glass. Not only can it be a focal point in a room (Fig. 7), but it can enliven a dark corner, dreary passage or hall. The light-box I illustrate is a dual-purpose frame which can either be artificially back-lit, standing on a table etc., or be placed on a window sill with the back removed, thus receiving natural light.

Fig. 8 shows the back of the light-box with the panel in its groove but the diffuser panel removed from its slot behind the stained glass. A diffuser is necessary as it hides and softens the source of artificial light, in this case two fluorescent strip lights, one on each side. A diffuser can be made of sandblasted glass or opaque perspex. The inside of the box is painted white to create maximum reflection. Fig. 9 shows the underneath of the light-box where the electrics are positioned, with the starters for both tubes.

FIXING A PANEL IN A DOOR

One of the most likely things you will wish to do when you have gained some experience in stained glass is to decorate a front or interior door or fanlight with stained glass. There are two problems associated with such a scheme if the panels are more than 610 sq mm (2 sq ft), or a long shape, such as 915mm (3ft) by 305mm (1ft). These larger areas tend to sag and must be strengthened; and with doors there is the added problem of movement, and impact, should they be banged.

There are two ways of strengthening such panels. The first is by using a special lead calm which has a steel rod running through the heart. This can be used on straight leads or gentle curves, but cannot be bent round extreme shapes. I have strengthened the vestibule panels in colour plate 1, using this special lead. The second possibility is the use of tie bars. These are metal bars which can be placed horizontally across the opening every 457mm (18in) or so, to which the panel is fixed with copper wire ties.

Measuring the aperture

If you want to design a panel for a given aperture, measure the *full size* of the opening. An aperture usually consists of a frame with a rebate. Measure right into the rebate (see Diags. 21a and b). However, it is better to be a fraction slack (1mm [$\frac{1}{32}$in]) on each side than too tight, because this will lead to problems in fitting.

fig. 8 The back of the light-box

fig. 9 The underneath of the light-box showing the circuitry

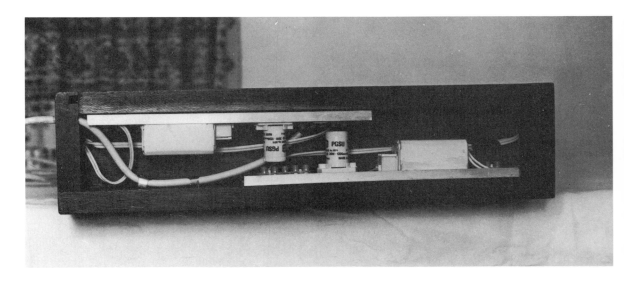

Inserting a panel

(This is applicable to small panels needing no strengthening, or those using the special lead.) Measure and cut the beading. Remove the old beading and the existing glass, and clean up the rebate. Try your panel for size: if too full, trim the outside lead; if slack, wedge with small pieces of wood. If you are glazing an *outside* door, put putty all along the rebate and press the panel into position. Hold it in position with panel pins, putty the beading and fix (see Diag. 21b).

Fixing a panel with a tie bar

A panel of the dimensions I have mentioned above can be strengthened with a tie bar. The panel should have been designed to accommodate the tie bar without spoiling the aesthetic effect. To be functional, the bar needs to be about midway down the panel. A metal bar 6mm ($\frac{1}{4}$in) in diameter is suitable – at least 50mm (2in) longer than the aperture. Measure the place where the ties are to be fixed across the panel, then solder copper ties onto each lead where the bar crosses it (see Diag. 21c). How these ties are spaced depends on the layout of the leads. Copper ties are made of stretched copper wire 100mm (4in) long, soldered in the middle to the respective leads (Diag. 21c)

Place the panel in position, line up the bar with the ties and mark on the door frame where the rod is to be fixed. Depending on how the rebate is positioned in the door, it can be in front of the panel or behind it. Remove the panel and drill two holes 50mm (2in) deep on one side, 25mm (1in) deep on the other: this will allow you to manoeuvre the bar into position. Put the bar in place, then the panel, and wedge it with some small bits of wood (matchsticks can sometimes work well) making sure that it cannot fall out. Bend the copper ties round the bar and, using a pair of pliers, twist each one to clamp it firmly. The ends must be trimmed off and pressed down neatly (Diag. 21d). Finally, the beading is nailed into position, with a hole cut into it to go round the bar, should it be on the same side as the beading.

diag. 21 Fixing a panel in a door

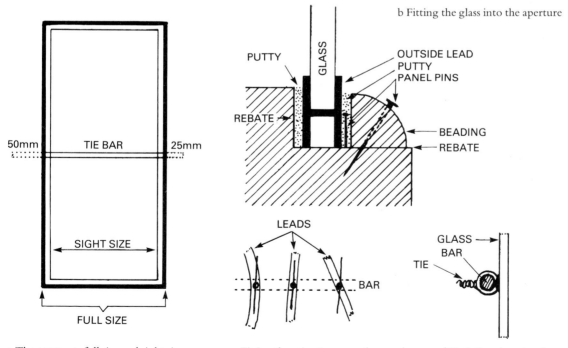

a The aperture: full size and sight size

c Fixing the wire ties on to the panel

d Twisting the wire tie round the bar

CHAPTER THREE

Introduction to glasspainting

Glasspainting is the most misunderstood and neglected of all the major techniques of stained glass. Since the 1960s, many commissions have been carried out without glasspainting, just using coloured glass and lead. I suspect that cost is an important reason for eliminating the process of glasspainting, for it is a time-consuming technique; the pigment must be fired in a kiln to make it permanent, and there is always the risk of the glass breaking in the firing. Then there is the question of fashion: the heavily-painted windows of the late nineteenth century caused a reaction against glasspainting. Windows were painted far more lightly, and fewer craftsmen were needed for glasspainting techniques; fewer apprentices were trained, and so finally this led to a shortage of skilled people able to undertake glasspainting commissions. In the last few years, however, I have noticed an upsurge of interest in glasspainting techniques among students anxious not only to appreciate the glasspainting of the past, but to produce painted work themselves.

The obvious reason for painting on glass is to depict the fundamental drawing lines. This process of painting the basic lines onto glass is called tracing – because you are painting details onto the glass from a cartoon beneath. These lines might indicate the features of a face: the eyes, nose or mouth; they might show the folds of drapery, or draw a pattern.

Glasspainting is also necessary when making an abstract window, in order to *control the light*. This second reason for glasspainting is as important as the first. Untreated coloured glass, even the most exceptional hand-made kind, still needs some glasspainting to bring out the quality of the colour. Leaving it unpainted is like singing in a raw tone, without modulating the voice. By this I don't mean that you should cover all the areas with pigment, but that you should consider the actual glass in a particular work and judge which parts will be enhanced by half-tone. You

can control what might be harsh, and bring out the beauty of quiet areas.

If you breathe on a window pane and draw a pattern in the film of condensation from your breath, you can quickly understand the process in glasspainting where we lay a matt of pigment on the glass, then work into it with various brushes, altering the matt by removing or modifying part of it, before the pigment is fired, to make it permanent. The light is filtered as it passes through the glass with this type of half-tone glasspainting on it, and makes the colour richer. The matts can be smooth traditional ones or modern textured kinds, but they all have the same function: to control the light.

REQUIREMENTS

Materials and sundries (the numbers refer to Diag. 22)

Pigment (4)

The medium used for glasspainting is a vitreous enamel, referred to in the craft as pigment. (Don't confuse this with coloured enamels.) Various shades of pigment are available, both tracing and shading colours, but for the beginner I advise 25–50g (0.9–1.8oz) of Shading Brown, which can be used as an all-purpose pigment.

Gum arabic (2), *sugar* (1) *or black treacle* (3)

All these three substances can be used to help the pigment flow. You must experiment and see which you prefer. Gum arabic comes in both powder and liquid form. Sugar or black treacle are to be used in tracing processes only.

Silver stain (8)

This oxide of silver is mixed with water and applied to the back of the glass to create gold tones. Buy Strong Silver Stain, 25–50g (0.9–1.8oz).

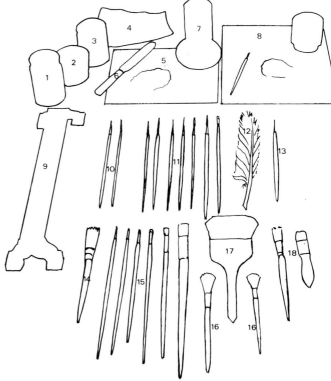

fig. 10 Requirements for glasspainting

Painting tile (5) and staining tile (8)
A glass square of 4mm ($\frac{1}{8}$in) glass, 229mm (9in) square, with dulled edges, on which to mix pigment. Ideally, a sandblasted surface is used for a mixing tile, but it is not essential. Have a separate tile for mixing stain.

A pigment cover
Use a terracotta plant pot base. Soak it in water for a few hours and cover your mixed pigment with it to keep it moist. It must be damp for as long as you want to keep the pigment ready for use.

A water pot (7)
Any jar will do.

Palette knife (6)
This springy knife is for mixing the pigment. You need one with a 152mm (6in) blade.

Tracing paper
This is needed for putting behind the painting easel to obscure the light.

Cloth
This will be used for cleaning the glass.

diag. 22 Key to Fig. 10, numbered: 1 Sugar 2 Liquid gum arabic 3 Black treacle 4 Pigment 5 Paint tile 6 Palette knife 7 Water pot 8 Stain tile, brush and water pot 9 Hand rest 10 Tracing brushes with short hair (21mm [$\frac{13}{16}$in]) 11 Seven tracing brushes specially made with long hair (35mm [1$\frac{3}{8}$in]) with pointed ends, except for the two on the right – one domed, the other chisel-ended 12 Quill 13 Needle 14 English stippler 15 Various scrubs 16 Two small badger brushes 17 Large badger brush 18 Flats or mops

Plasticine
Use this for sticking the pieces of glass to be painted upon the glass easel.

Plaster of Paris
This is for laying on the kiln batt so that the glass will not stick to it. Standard packs are available.

Painting equipment

Painting easel (Diag. 23)
This is required for half-tone work. Standing on this wooden easel is a sheet of 3–4mm ($\frac{2}{16}$–$\frac{3}{16}$in) glass taped round the edges. All the pieces of glass needing half-tone treatment will be stuck up on this glass easel and painted against the light.

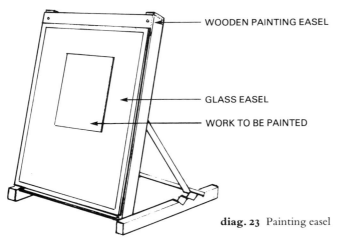

WOODEN PAINTING EASEL

GLASS EASEL

WORK TO BE PAINTED

diag. 23 Painting easel

Hand rest (9)

This is a wooden bridge, 304mm (12in) long on two feet (wooden blocks) 76mm (3in) high. You need this rest on which to balance your wrist while tracing.

Mawl stick

This is a 120–150cm (4–5ft) cane used to rest your arm on while painting.

fig. 11 Using a hand rest while tracing: note the long-haired rigger brush

Tracing brushes (11)

Try using your ordinary painting brushes; but I recommend specialist brushes for the best results: size one or two. The traditional long-haired, long-handled tracing brushes called riggers are usually made of light ox hair or sable. They have a springiness and flexibility which can achieve a most expressive line as soon as you are used to them. I have mine specially made with hair 35mm ($1\frac{3}{8}$in) long – the average is 21mm ($\frac{13}{16}$in)

Half-toning brushes
Mop (or flat) (18)

This is a wide brush which takes up a lot of moisture, for laying on a matt. You need one 25mm (1in) wide.

Badger (16 and 17)

This is a firm but soft wide brush, used for smoothing the pigment into silk or stipple matts. As the hairs are genuine, a large badger brush will cost more than £40; but you can buy one 38mm ($1\frac{1}{2}$in) wide which is quite adequate for small-scale work, costing a third of the price.

Scrubs (15)

These stiff, hog-hair brushes are for taking out the highlights; they are oil-painting brushes and have to be adapted for stained glass use. Don't cut their bristles: heat up an old knife and singe the hair to the shape required, then sandpaper the ends smooth. If you are doing much glasspainting, you will need various widths of scrub.

Staining brush

An ordinary brush, size 2 or 3. Keep it for staining only.

Quill (12)

A goose quill is the strongest.

Needle (13)

Stick the head into the end of an old brush handle.

The kiln (Fig. 12)

In recent years, smaller electric stained glass kilns have become available (see List of Suppliers). Alternatively, you could use an enamelling or pottery kiln. Some enamelling kilns are reasonably portable, and run off a 13 amp socket. For much of my work I find it economical to use two enamelling kilns, one as a firing chamber, the other for annealing. The annealing process, warming the glass slowly and controlling its cooling rate, is very important, as otherwise the glass will crack. The muffle (chamber) of my kiln is 304mm (12in) × 304mm (12in) × 102mm (4in).

fig. 12 Firing in the kiln: there are two small kilns, the second one used as an annealing chamber. The metal boxes on top are for stacking trays of glass before firing and after annealing

Preparing the kiln for firing

You will need a thin (7mm [¼in]) ceramic batt (shelf) on which to lay your work to be fired. This cannot sit on the floor of the kiln but must have air underneath, so you must purchase little stilts on which to stand it. These items can be bought from a pottery supplier.

You cannot lay your glass to be fired directly onto the batt because it might stick. A layer of 'dead' (i.e. with the moisture removed) plaster of Paris must be applied. You must prepare this plaster before you want to fire for the first time; then keep some in stock. Pile a heap of plaster of Paris on the batt and put it in your kiln. Turn the thermostat to 650°C (1202°F); when it has reached that temperature, turn off the kiln and leave the plaster to cool. You must always make your plaster 'dead' or else it will mark the glass on the first firing. Keep your prepared plaster in a special sealed container.

PAINTING TECHNIQUES

Preparation of pigment for tracing

The mixing of pigment is traditionally part of the whole discipline of producing a brush line, connecting the technique of tracing with the great traditions of calligraphy, Western and Eastern. Far-Eastern exponents (who produce calligraphy with a brush, not a pen) spend at least half-an-hour grinding and mixing their ink. They consider that the rhythmic action of preparing the medium is a focusing of concentration, a building-up of a sense of rhythm, not a chore they would prefer to avoid. Bear this idea in mind when you mix your pigment. The process of tracing begins with the mixing of the pigment, not the first brushline (although modern pigment has been finely ground and does not require the amount of mixing it did in the old days). (See Health & Safety, page 116.)

Fix your glass mixing-tile onto your work-surface by putting a little blob of plasticine in the four corners underneath the tile and pressing down so that it does not slip about. Take a heaped teaspoon of pigment and place it in the centre of the tile. Grind the dry pigment with your palette knife for a little; then put a little water in the middle of the pigment and mix it to a smooth paste with the palette knife. Keep flipping the paste into the centre of the tile. Then take a small amount of sugar (or black treacle or gum arabic) on the tip of a teaspoon and mix this in. Be careful not to put too much or else the paint will fry in the firing. The sugar (or the other substance, whichever you have preferred) helps the pigment to flow off the brush; it also makes it firm on the glass, so that if you have got to transport your painted work to a kiln, it will not brush off easily if covered. Keep grinding the mixture into the centre of the tile and, when it is perfectly smooth, gather it up into the centre of the tile and keep it moist and clean by covering it with the dampened terracotta

lid. It will keep for weeks if it remains damp; and even if you let it dry out, you can regrind it. It is a specialist substance, costly, and you never need throw any away.

Free tracing exercises (Fig. 13)

Take a sheet of window glass about 304mm (12in) square and clean it. The pigment will not adhere if there is any grease on the surface. Just breathe on the glass and polish it with a clean cloth. If it is dirty, put a spot of pigment on it and rub it round – it acts as a rouge – then clean it off. Have your pigment tile conveniently near your sheet of glass. Lay the glass on a piece of white paper on your table. Dip your tracing brush in water, shake off the excess, then roll it in the pigment; but do not push the ferrule onto the tile, as you might cut off some hairs. Then put your rest across the glass and lean your wrist on it. It will feel odd at first, but it is an essential support: your wrist must be steadied, as the movement of the brush is governed by the action of the fingers.

Draw several lines to get the feel of the brush on the glass. When you first try to paint a line, you will find it is difficult to judge exactly when your tip arrives at the surface of the glass, because your eyes are conditioned to focus on the paper under the glass. You will arrive sooner than you thought and the brush will make a little blob at the beginning of your line. With practice you will eliminate this bad start. Painting on glass is quite different from painting on paper – the glass is not absorbent. If you want your line to be thick, use more pressure; if you want it thinner, release the pressure on the brush. You can get a whole range of strokes, from very thin to really thick on *one* brush. Keep practising. Wipe off all you have done and start again, trying to produce an expressive line. The essence of good tracing is a *feeling* for line. A line is a living, elastic movement. When you practise painting lines, think of branches and flowing movements – waves and clouds. Notice that the density of the pigment will vary: this gives life and interest to a line. However, if you want a solid, dark effect, you may paint over it as long as the line is still moist. You must *not* go over a line if it has dried, as this build-up of pigment can flake off when fired.

Practise free tracing regularly so that you master spontaneous effects. A laboured line will always spoil your work. Practise lines of varying density: the more water on the tip of your brush, mixed on the edge of the pigment pool to dilute it, the washier the line.

Making tracing samples

Make a number of small tracing samples on clear glass before you attempt Project 7. In this way you will find

fig. 13 Tracing and painting techniques: small handsamples

diag. 24 Tracing lines demonstrating how variation in thickness of line controls the light

out what happens to the pigment during firing. It is wise to get a little experience of firing and the characteristics of your kiln before embarking on work you have lavished much effort on; for it is discouraging to spoil it, and the commonest fault with beginners is to rush ahead without adequate groundwork. Investing time in firing batches of small samples at this stage will be repaid by excellent results on larger projects later on (see p.42). I suggest you make a number of tracing samples based on Diag. 24, which shows how varying thicknesses of tracing line can distribute the light across a piece of glass.

Looking after your brushes

Respect your brushes. Don't leave them in a water pot, as they will go out of shape. Don't leave a brush in the pigment, because it sets hard and when you come to pick the brush up you will rip out some hairs. Always wash and dry your brushes carefully, smooth them into shape and stand them in a pot, hairs up.

PROJECT 7: 'The Green Man'

Make an enlargement of the subject provided and put it on your table. Place your piece of glass (plain or coloured, as you prefer) cut to the correct size, on top of the cartoon, and trace the lines you can see through onto the glass. But remember that tracing is not just making a slavish copy: it must have life – it is a reinterpretation of the tracing subject. If you have knowledge of drawing, it is a great advantage both for tracing and half-tone techniques. Study your cartoon, think out your interpretation, planning where you intend the nuances of line; then paint without hesitation.

This subject of the Green Man needs bold treatment. The lines should be black, so go over them as long as the pigment on the glass is still moist. If, however, the pigment is now dry, you must be content to fire it, and give it a second painting and firing (see p.43) to achieve the added density. You can use the end of your brush handle, sharpened to a point, to scratch out any irregularities in your line, but this must not be overdone, as the line will lose its authenticity if tampered with more than a little. You can turn your

diag. 25 Tracing Project 7: 'The Green Man' – a popular medieval subject thought to be a fertility god connected with tree worship. Reduced cartoon.

cartoon round and replace the glass on top if you find certain areas difficult to do in the position you began with. Trace difficult lines, especially curves, at the most comfortable angle. Be prepared to wipe off all you have painted and start again. All my students know that I insist on much practice – ten times is not unusual. How many times does a fine musician play a phrase to make it perfect? It is the same with glasspainting

FIRING TRACED WORK

To make the pigment permanent, the glass must now be fired in a kiln at 620–650°C (1148–1202°F). Any kiln can be used, but obviously firing a small piece in a large kiln is uneconomical. Before placing the glass on the ceramic batt, it must be prepared by putting a layer of dead plaster of Paris on it. Lay a thick newspaper on the table, put the batt on it, then shake some dead plaster through a sieve, making a thin layer approximately 3mm ($\frac{1}{8}$in) thick. Take another newspaper and lay it gently on top, smoothing it with your hand so that the surface of the plaster is level. The heated glass will pick up any mark on the plaster, so it must be perfectly smooth and flat. Lay your piece of glass on the batt. If you are firing more than one piece, see that they do not touch. Place the batt in the kiln on the supports which lift it off the floor.

Firing procedure

Close the kiln door and turn on the thermostat to 650°C (1202°F). As it approaches 610°C (1130°F), it is advisable to start checking the glass. Your aim is to fire the pigment into the glass, which ideally should have a lightly-polished surface. The shape of the glass should not alter: if it does, you are firing much too hot; and this overheating will cause the pigment to fire away. Just as every cook knows that each oven has its peculiarities, and cannot rely on good results until the vagaries of a particular oven are known and taken into consideration, so you must get to know your kiln and its characteristics.

I cannot give a set temperature at which your pigment will fire into the glass. It depends on the kiln, the type of glass, and the pigment you have used. It is usually about 650°C (1202°F); but it is better to underfire it slightly. At about 610°C (1130°F) the glass is usually a dull red and the pigment a darkish brown; at 620°C (1148°F) the glass is redder and the pigment still visible. When the pigment reaches its firing temperature, the lines will disappear as it becomes gloss. You must observe these changes to become adept at firing, but take care when you open the kiln, just as you do when opening the oven door, for the blast of escaping air is very hot.

fig. 14 'Pelican in Piety' based on a window border in the Latin Chapel, Christ Church Cathedral, Oxford (reproduced by permission of the Dean and Chapter)

With regard to turning the kiln off at the right moment, take the analogy of boiling milk: you have to remove the milk from the heat just *before* it is fully boiling, or else it will boil over. Just so with firing glass: you have to turn off the kiln at, say, 630–640°C (1166–1184°F), *just before* the optimum firing temperature of around 650°C (1202°F). In the large stained glass studios which have big kilns with annealing chambers, when the glass becomes cherry red at about 650°C (1202°F), it is removed from the heat and put in the cooling chamber. Most individuals do not have such facilities, however, so the glass has to be left in the kiln to anneal. That is why it is essential to turn off the kiln *just before* the required temperature, as, when it is turned off, the kiln will continue to get hotter for a little while, before it registers the effects of the turn-off. Firing is calculated guesswork. Your eye and your firing skills will develop through experience. I would stress the importance of making a few small test-firings before you fire your Green Man, if you want to be quite sure not to spoil it.

Second firing

Allow the kiln to cool for at least 12 hours before you open it and remove your project. Wipe the plaster off and hold it to the light. If you feel that any traced areas are weak or too thin, you can trace over the necessary parts and refire. You will also realise that in every firing a small part of the pigment fires away. If you are determined to aim for a specific effect, you will often have to do a second painting and firing.

Suggested subjects for traced panels (these can also be stained, see p. 48)

Religious motifs

Figs. 14 and 15 show traced panels with a religious emphasis. 'Pelican in Piety' is based on a border of a mid fourteenth-century window in the Latin Chapel, Christ Church Cathedral, Oxford. In Christian symbolism this subject denotes love: the pelican pierces her breast to nurture her young ones. This panel has been traced, then the beak and feet stained a rich gold and fired; a pale wash stain was then applied to the body and fired at a lower temperature. 'The Pilgrims of the Canterbury Tales' is a facsimile of a subject in Caxton's first edition with woodcuts, 1485. The woodcut has required a flexible and washy tracing line.

Initials

A panel incorporating an initial is an attractive, personalised gift. Choose an initial from a calligraphy book, or design your own. Trace it onto your glass, paying special attention to the thick and thin lines which will give the letter(s) rhythm and life. When

fig. 15 'The Pilgrims of the Canterbury Tales' (reproduced by permission of the Master and Fellows of Magdalene College, Cambridge)

you become more skilled, a letter based on an illuminated example from the medieval period, probably containing animal grotesques and foliage, makes an interesting subject.

Zodiac signs
Simple versions of zodiac signs, based on originals or designed by yourself, are motifs which lend themselves to tracing, and which are acceptable presents.

Tracing on the 'Wheatears' panel (Project 5)
If you wish your wheatear pieces to have a naturalistic, curved appearance, trace the outline of a wheatear on the rectangular shape of the glass, filling in the whole of the area outside the wheatear shape with pigment, as illustrated in Diag. 18. Fire all these pieces in the kiln. When the panel is glazed, the eye will pick up the curved outline of the pigment, not the stylised lead line.

HALF-TONE PAINTING TECHNIQUES

Preparing the pigment

Grind the pigment with the palette knife, then add a little gum arabic; if it is in powder form, also add a little water then mix well to a smooth, quite runny consistency and test. Using a mop, put a little on a piece of scrap glass held in the hand, and badger to make it smooth. When it is dry, take a scrub and make a mark. If it is too soft the pigment will come off easily; but if you have put too much gum arabic in, the pigment will be very difficult to remove. It is a matter of

personal preference as to how soft the matt you work in should be; it depends on the effect you require and the skill you develop on handling it. The less gum you use, the more difficult it is to work in, because it is so soft. Only experience will teach you the right amount of gum to use. I recommend you make a sample of each of the techniques below on small pieces of clear glass before embarking on a project.

Creating a silk matt

Take your cleaned glass sample piece and stick it up on your painting easel glass with a little Plasticine placed all round its under edge, gently pressing it on the base glass so that it adheres and balances properly. Blobs of hot beeswax were used in the old days, but plasticine is much more convenient nowadays.

Mix your pigment containing gum arabic into the centre of the tile. Dip your clean mop in water and take up some pigment from the edge of the amount – you don't want it too dense. Test the weight of the pigment on the base glass of the easel: you want a middle tone (and remember that it will darken as it dries). Lay the matt in lines from top to bottom all over the glass *as evenly as possible*. Work quickly, as the pigment will already be drying. It should not run. If it does, you have too much water on the brush. Take up the badger and, with a wrist movement, lightly draw the brush across the paint, trying to even it out as much as possible – you may move the brush in all directions *very lightly*. Use the tip only: if you press, it will go streaky. The pigment dries from the edges inwards.

Creating a stipple matt

On your next piece of sample glass, lay a matt as described above, then smooth it over with the badger to even out the pigment. Then punch the surface with the tip of the badger brush to create a stippled effect. If you want a fine stipple, continue to badger so that the pigment becomes drier, then punch into it – this creates a soft grain. A bold stipple can be produced by working into it when the matt is more moist.

Use of the mawl stick

For the following techniques you need something to steady your hand. Just as easel painters do, you must use a mawl stick. This is a 120–150cm (4–5ft) cane held in the left hand and placed across the easel so that the right hand with the brush is supported.

Removing highlights

With scrubs and sticks
Matt a piece of sample glass and make a silk or stipple matt. Then take a scrub and experiment with various

lines, seeing how much pressure you need to remove or modify the pigment. When you use a pointed end of a stick (or sharpened end of a tracing brush) a sharp line is made, which can be used in picked-out patterns.

With quills and needles
Take a piece of sample glass, and practise working on a matt with a quill. It gives a beautiful flexible line because the tip is sensitive to pressure, and marvellous flourishes can be made. A needle produces the finest line for delicate effects and subtle work, especially on faces, but its line is of one thickness; pressure will not vary it.

Fire all your samples to make them permanent.

Modern half-tone techniques

A great variety of striking textures can be created with modern techniques. Work directly onto the glass, dabbing pigment on with a sponge. This can be modified by manipulating it so that it shows finger marks. Pigment can be applied with different sizes of toothbrush or dabbed on with screwed-up paper. Splattering of pigment can be most effective. You can invent ways of your own to express yourself in glasspainting. Make a variety of samples and fire them.

Water-spotted matts are among my favourites: lay a stipple matt on the glass, let it dry, then flick water on it. When this is completely dry, rub your fingers over the area very lightly and bubble shapes will appear where the water has affected the matt. A panel using modern glasspainting methods can be seen in Fig. 30.

PROJECT 8: 'The Country Lane'
Cutting and glazing pp. 28–30

The cutline for this panel is Diag. 17. The reduced working cartoon shows the lines to be traced. Fig. 16 shows the finished panel. I have used streaky rolled cathedral glass for all areas except the sunrays: these are in waterglass which has a rippled light-catching surface. My glasspainting has allowed for the particular patterning and textures of the glass: you can adapt your tracing and painting to the characteristics of your glass.

Functions of tracing lines

There are two kinds of tracing line in this project:

Painted lead lines
These are strong, dense lines delineating form around which the leads are glazed. They must be painted around *some* parts of the glass shapes, according to their prominence in the design. For example, look at piece *24*: this shows a wavy silhouette representing the tops of distant trees on the hillside. The leadline alone cannot possibly show these complicated shapes, so this silhouette is painted along its top within the glass shape so that when the glass is fitted into its lead you can still see it. At no time must the leaf of the lead obscure this painted line. Look at *19*: this foliage shape is in front of all the other foliage shapes. You make the eye understand its prominence by painting a dense line all round its outline. This line, of varying width, can give a subtlety to the shape which the lead cannot do. These painted lead lines are also used to emphasise the rays of the sun and other prominent features in the design, such as the sweep of the lane leading the eye upwards.

Internal drawing lines
These traced lines delineate all the details you want to show such as grass, plants, foliage clusters etc. They can vary in density from very washy to black, according to your personal taste; but variety of tracing line will give the panel life and interest.

Tracing the project

1 Lay glass pieces *1, 7* and *10* on the working cartoon. They must be placed accurately, their edges running along the middle of the black lead line. If you do not position your glass correctly, some painting will be obliterated by the leaf of the lead. Trace the lines of the tree trunk on *7*: these parallel lines indicate the important subject of the trunk which stands out from the background. Keep *7* in position and trace *1*, making sure that the lines run through. Paint details on the top from left to right all along, except for the part which shows the tree bole. Piece *10* has a lead line painted on each side, next to *9* and *11*. Remove these three pieces and place them on the cutline: check the lines of *1* and *7* run through. If you are not satisfied, wipe off and trace again

2 Pieces *2, 14, 15, 16*. Paint a lead line all along the top of each piece. Trace the internal drawing lines with varying densities. On *15*, paint a lead line down each side as well as across the top.

3 Pieces *3, 23* and *24*. Paint the lead lines on the top delineating the wavy silhouette of the trees.

4 Tree foliage areas: pieces *12, 13, 19, 20, 21*. Paint a lead line along the bottom of *12*. Piece *13* is in front of *12*, so paint a lead line from top left-hand (under piece *20*) to bottom right-hand (piece *19*) to help the cluster appear to be in front. Check that the branch on *13* is in line with *10*. *19* has a strong lead line painted all the way round it. *21* has a painted line on the left and right sides; *20* has a line along the bottom. All the inner drawing lines should vary in density to add interest. For a softer

line add a little water to the tip of your brush before picking up the pigment.

5 Treatment of sun and rays: pieces *4, 6, 8, 11, 17, 25, 27, 29, 31, 33*. Dense lead lines are painted on each side of every ray to help them stand out from the sky. The curve of the sun has a lead line. Delicately trace stylised ray lines along the length of the rays.

Firing the project: tracing stage

Fire all pieces according to firing instructions on p. 42.

Preparation for half-toning

Clean each piece with a soft cloth. Put the cutline on the table and place the glass easel on it. Stick all the pieces of glass to the glass easel with a neat application of Plasticine all along the under edges of the pieces. Make sure that all the pieces are placed accurately on the cutline within the black line which represents the heart of the lead. Prepare the wooden easel frame by sticking tracing paper across the back to soften the light during painting. (You may prop your sheet of glass on a window sill if you haven't got an easel, but take care it doesn't slip down. Fix a sheet of tracing paper to the back of the sheet after carrying out the following process of applying artificial lead lines.) You will note that there is a gap in between all the glass pieces where the heart of the lead will go. I advise you to turn the sheet of glass round and paint all the artificial lead lines on the back, using black powder paint with a little black treacle added. This gives the effect of what the panel will look like finished, because the colours come

diag. 26 'The Country Lane' – reduced cartoon showing a possible tracing treatment. For painting, enlarge to same size as cutline.

fig. 16 Project 8: 'The Country Lane' illustrating the finished painting

together when joined by the black lines. Don't wash them off the back until after the second painting. You can also mask out the sides of the panel with brown paper fixed to the front of the glass sheet if you want to get the full effect of the colours which you intend to treat with half-tone.

THE HALF-TONING PROCESS

My half-toning on the illustrated panel is just to show you how I have treated my glass. It is up to you how you treat your matting on the glass you have chosen. All glass is unique and must be treated individually.

Testing the pigment

Mix your pigment with some gum arabic: aim to get a pigment which is fairly stiff. Test it on a piece of scrap white glass. Lay on a matt, smooth a few times with a badger, then stipple while the pigment is still wet: this will create a bold stipple. Do not over-stipple. When the pigment begins to dry, your stipple effect becomes too fine, with pinpoints of light coming through, because you are removing, not redistributing, the pigment. Allow the stipple matt to dry, then test by rubbing your middle finger gently over the surface of the paint. If the pigment is too soft, you will remove it

in one touch. You need to be able to keep stroking the surface of the paint gently so that the dark blobbing remains where it is, but the light dotting is removed. This gives you the texture you require for this panel. Also, the actual texture of the glass will be revealed too: this can be clearly seen on the foliage areas in the photograph.

Carrying out the half-toning

1 Work from the top downwards. Your aim is to modify the light coming through the glass, removing the matts by degrees. You don't want extremes but varying tones with highlights here and there of pure glass: this will bring out its intrinsic beauty.

2 Stipple matt all areas except the sun rays. If you get some pigment on the sun rays, it can be removed with a scrub when dry.

3 Silk matt the sun rays. This demands skill because you must not get pigment on the other pieces you have already matted, nor remove pigment from elsewhere. Don't get the matt too wet or else it will transfer to other areas.

4 Start to bring out the texture by rubbing your middle finger on the dry matt on the foliage areas. Take a scrub and brush it over the lighter parts to create highlights. You can use the sharpened end of the tracing brush handle to create sticklights – these can indicate leaf effects, for example. Use your mawl stick when using scrubs or sticks to balance your hand.

5 Continue working on all other stippled areas. Take the scrub and lightly remove some of the matt all down the right side of the tree trunk, taking care not to get too harsh an effect.

6 Draw delicate sticklights down the sunrays to make them catch the light.

7 Consider how to treat the sky background between the sunrays. This depends on the nature of the glass you have used. If you have chosen streaky glass, enhance the streaks by reinforcing their shapes with paint: you can see that I have done this on my panel. You will probably remove more of the stipple matt on the sky areas than anywhere else, as this is the clearest part of the panel.

8 Remove your tracing paper and consider where to put your final highlights. You may like to remove a little more pigment from the lightest areas, to give the work sparkle.

9 Lay the glass sheet on the table and lift off all the pieces of glass. Carefully remove all Plasticine from the backs, rolling it into a ball to use again. Be sure you have cleaned off all traces with a cloth, but take care of your paintwork.

Firing the first painting

Fire all the pieces.

10 Stick up the panel again without using the tracing paper on the easel. Consider which areas need further painting. This is up to you; but the second painting will give a richness and definition, because paint fires away in the kiln. When you get very skilled you will know how to compensate for this by painting a little more heavily; but even so, a perfectionist will not be satisfied with one painting unless oil-matt techniques are employed, which are beyond the scope of these chapters. Unless you have overfired your pieces, you should not have to completely re-matt all your pieces, but merely reinforce certain areas you want defined or richer in texture.

Firing the second painting

Fire all the repainted pieces. The pieces are now ready for glazing (see p. 30).

STAINING TECHNIQUES

How confusing the term 'stained' glass is for the general public. 'Do you stain your own glass?' is the question I frequently get asked when I am demonstrating at craft events. I have to explain that stained glass artists buy stained, i.e. coloured, glass from the specialist manufacturer. But there is a specific process of staining using oxide of silver (silver nitrate), discovered in the early fourteenth century, which colours glass yellow. Tones of stain can vary from the palest lemon to the deepest bronzy brown according to the type and amount of stain used, the kind of glass and the temperature of the kiln. There are various strengths of stain on the market: I advise a beginner to buy Strong Silver Stain and to experiment with thickness of application to obtain a range of tone. Stain is traditionally applied to the *back* of the glass, leaving the front for pigment. It is fired at a lower temperature than pigment: 520–550°C (968–1022°F). I recommend you fire your stain after you have fired your pigment: you need to be very experienced to fire pigment and stain simultaneously.

Applying silver stain

Dry-grind half a teaspoonful of stain on a glass tile used for stain only. Add a little water and work up into a paste with your palette knife: it must be of a smooth consistency. After you have mixed your stain, clean the knife thoroughly straight away, otherwise it will corrode. Take your stain brush and take up a little stain from the edge of the amount.

Take a piece of plain sample glass and try drawing bands of stain along it with different amounts on the brush. Then make a big blob of it in another place. If you want a larger area of stain, mix a wetter mixture on the tile, put it on a sample glass and shake it so that it spreads evenly over a large area: this creates a varying density of colour which is interesting. You can also badger the stain to make it even; but your brush must be thoroughly washed after using stain, and ideally you should have a badger brush solely for staining. All these methods need practice so that you can discover the beauties of stain and how you would like to use it.

Firing stain

Stain tone becomes stronger the hotter you fire it; but if the glass is very sensitive, you might find it will be strong even at a lower temperature. The hand-made tinted white glasses are sensitive to stain. Usually, the greener the tint, the more sensitive it is. Firing principles for stain are the same as for firing pigment. Aim to turn the kiln off just before the optimum firing temperature. Get experience by making samples. After firing (leave to cool for at least 12 hours) it is essential to remove the plaster on which the stained piece has been resting, as there is a residue of oxide in the plaster which will transfer to any other work you place on the batt. Scoop out the plaster in that particular area and throw it away.

Staining simple projects

The tracing subjects such as initials and zodiac signs suggested as simple tracing projects are suitable for staining. After you have fired the tracing, clean up and apply stain on the back of the panel. If you want to try for the effect of two tones of stain on one subject, such as a golden lion with a tawny mane and tail, representing the zodiac sign for Leo, you would have to apply a thick layer of stain on the tawny parts and fire at the hotter end of the firing temperature, then fire for the second time at the lower end, having painted on a diluted wash of stain for a soft gold effect. I must stress that it is only experience that will enable you to fire stain with accuracy.

There is an added problem with the firing: in firing pigment you can peep into the kiln and see it changing as the temperature rises, but with stain you cannot unless your work is on trays that can be removed from the kiln and viewed from above. Looking across stained work on a batt in the kiln, you cannot see any changes, so you rely on making samples and notes to find out at what temperature your particular kiln produces a certain tone, dependent on the amount of stain you have applied. Traditionally, stained work is laid onto the batt with the painted side up and the stain side down.

CHAPTER FOUR

Developing skills in glasspainting

This chapter is divided into six sections, each illustrating, and describing in detail, a particular subject. You are encouraged to choose your own subject and carry it out, using the explanation of my subjects as the guide for yours. I am assuming that you have practised and assimilated all the basic techniques described in Chapter 3 before graduating to the advanced work discussed here.

AN ANIMAL STUDY (OR PAINTING YOUR PET) (Colour plate 2)

The processes detailed in the commentary on my panel 'Elgar the Enigma' will enable you to make a similar study. The building-up of the animal study is the same as for a portrait of a person.

Preparation of the cartoon

Take a good, detailed photograph of the subject, preferably the same size as the actual panel to be painted (otherwise you must enlarge your cartoon after you have prepared it). Place tracing paper over it and, using a soft pencil (2B) so that when you put pressure on it you get a thicker line, start to draw the main outlines of the subject, *thinking in terms of glass*. Always remember that, when preparing a cartoon for glass, you must consider from the very beginning the effect of halation: the way the light erodes a line. A line held against the light seems to be thinner than it actually is, so you must always compensate for this by making the line a little thicker.

After all the fundamental drawing lines, you must consider where the half-tone areas, which express form, must come, and indicate these on the cartoon. Every detail you want to put on the glass must be indicated in this working drawing or considered at this stage. People are surprised that you don't work direct

from the photograph when tracing, but this is inadvisable because you need to interpret all the lines in a way suitable for glasspainting before you begin tracing. You may, of course, use the photograph as an aid to glasspainting at the half-tone stage.

Consider the border you are going to use to frame your subject. It can be a single lead calm, or you may prefer to put a coloured border round it, as I have. Work out its dimensions and the type of decoration, if required. Decide on the width of the lead. Indicate all these details on the cartoon, then make a cutline from it. I recommend good-quality glass on which to paint your subject. White 'antique' hand-made glass, which although termed white is always slightly greenish in tone, takes stain well and also has slight reams which give it character.

Tracing the subject (Fig. 17)

Cut the glass panel on which to paint the subject; you can also cut the borders now, unless you prefer to judge the best tones in relation to the central panel after it has been painted. Place the cleaned glass over the cartoon with the photograph nearby for further reference. Proceed to trace the subject. You are aiming for quality of brushline. In my portrait of the cat, note the variation in thickness of the line round each ear and round the paw. Notice how the broken outlines of the brush strokes show the form of the ruff. The same type of brushstroke is used to create the distinctive tiger markings on the head. There are also some delicately-traced areas under the eyes which will help to plot and emphasise the contrast between the white border round the eyes and the darker fur.

You are endeavouring, with every brushstroke, to give a feeling of spontaneity which will give the work verve and character. This is achieved by an understanding of the subject and practice of technique. You

fig. 17 'Elgar the Enigma': trace lines

fig. 18 'Elgar the Enigma': commencing the half-toning – working out of the stipple matt

should be prepared to wipe off any lines you are not satisfied with and do them again and again ... No matter how experienced you are, you should be anxious to be even better.

Particularly important, in this cat panel, are the whiskers. These lines must be done without hesitation as they express so much of a cat's nature. To indicate the top line of a whisker, cut through the pigment with a needle: this can be seen clearly on the top right-hand whisker as it goes through the ruff. This must be done at this stage because once the tracing is fired, the pigment cannot be removed.

There is a technique of working on unfired lines (in fact, this cat has been painted this way). This means that when you have finished tracing, you do not fire it but proceed to the half-tone techniques. You can still modify the traced lines and take out any highlights, as the pigment is still unfired. However, this technique is only suitable for the highly-experienced glasspainter, as the risk of ruining the work is high. If you should make a serious mistake during half-toning, you will have to begin again completely from scratch.

The focal point of the cat panel is the eyes. These must hypnotise you! I have painted the pupils on the *back* of the glass, which gives an uncanny effect of depth. The eyes seem to follow you as you walk by the panel. The highlight in each eye is done with the point of a stick, and is called a sticklight. It is essential for all but the very experienced glasspainters to fire the panel at this stage to make the tracing permanent.

Half-toning (Figs. 17, 18)

Stick the fired panel up on the glass easel. The big blobs of Plasticine in Fig. 18 are in addition to the edging of Plasticine all round the under edge of the panel, and are an extra precaution against the panel slipping off the easel.

Stipple-matt the whole surface of the glass and allow it to dry. You then start to work on the lightest areas first, working back into the tones. A scrub removes some of the matt, with a stroking motion, to create the effect of white fur on the chest, the paw, round the eyes and ears. Don't remove too much of the matt at this

fig. 19 'Elgar the Enigma': end of the first painting

fig. 20 'Elgar the Enigma': applying the stronger stain – on the back of the panel

stage: your perfectly white areas are reserved for the highlights. The scrub is also used on the nose with a light punching action to give smooth gradations of tone, and showing the different texture of very short fur. It also helps to build up an effect of form. Then all the other areas are worked on to bring out the particular shape.

After this I added dark touches of pigment on the tip of the tracing brush (testing it out on the glass easel), especially in the tiger markings, to bring out the contrasting tones in the fur. The distinctive marks of the quill are clearly visible in the white fur on the chest, and the use of the needle is illustrated in the delicate lines on the foreleg, under the chin, in the ears and in the two lines above the ears on the brow. Sticklights emphasise the shape of the ears. A scrub and needle have created subtle effects on the iris of the eyes, following the form. Finally, the whisker highlights have been put in: those on the big whiskers with a quill, which gives a line of varying thickness; and those on the small whiskers with a needle. The panel is then fired.

Second firing

Pigment tends to fire away: the hotter the firing, the paler it will be. I stipple-matted the background again and put small areas of stipple where I felt the contrast in tones was lacking. These were then worked on with a scrub and needle to soften the edges and make the second application of matt settle into the overall effect. A little blue enamel has been applied to the carpet pattern below the cat's foreleg, but this delicate tone does not show up well on the photograph.

Staining

I had to make two stain firings: the first one at about 560°C (1040°F) to achieve the richer tones; the second at about 520°C (968°F) to fire the paler tints (the range of stain tone can only be appreciated on the original). The back of the panel shown in Fig. 20 illustrates what was applied in the first stain firing. The stain has been badgered in parts, as you can see by the uneven outline of certain patches, such as top left below the ear. In the second stain application, a thin layer of pale stain was

fig. 21 'The Matron': trace lines

fig. 22 'The Matron': after the first painting

fig. 23 'The Matron': finished painting (top); 'Westminster Hospital': finished painting (bottom) – on the glass easel, before glazing

painted on and modified in some parts with a scrub; then the highlights, such as whiskers, were picked out.

Painting the border

This has a traced beading, on to which a silk matt was applied and modified with a scrub and sticklights to give tonal variety. In the areas where the matt has been removed, the blue appears brighter; where the blue appears darker the matt is controlling the light passing through the glass.

PAINTING A PORTRAIT

A portrait of family members, perhaps made on roundels, is not only a valuable personal record but an heirloom. Such work demands knowledge of drawing, form and anatomy, as well as glasspainting techniques, but you can work towards mastering the skills necessary for good portrait work. Figs. 21–23 illustrate my portrait of the Matron of Westminster Hospital, 1915–48, part of a memorial window designed by Francis Skeat, FMGP, made in 1982. Four stages of my work are shown with a detailed commentary to help you understand the building-up of such a study.

'The Matron'

I was given a photograph of the subject, and from this I made a working drawing, interpreting all the main drawing lines for glasspainting. Fig. 21 shows the small scale on which I was required to work. At this tracing stage I was trying to capture with my brush the different qualities of line required by the delineation of the eyes, eyebrows and nose; the lighter lines of the starched cap; the stronger tracing of the furniture, and so on. Before firing the tracing I put a silk matt on the back of the glass – on the curtains, table and books – and took out the highlights with scrubs and needles.

The portrait at the end of the first firing is shown in Fig. 22. I matted the entire surface with a silk matt and worked into the tones with a scrub, lightly punching the matt – this treatment can clearly be seen behind the head. The matron's uniform has been worked on in the same way, then the lighter areas carried out by stroking movements of the scrub and needle. The grain of the desk is done in the same way. Parts of the wire letter tray have been picked out with a needle. The darker areas, which were back-painted, have had further half-toning work on the front. Fig. 23 shows the portrait after the second painting in which the usual adjustments have been made to compensate for the loss of

For God & the Empire

pigment in firing. I applied a blue-black pigment to the uniform. The chair and desk were then lightly stained.

ARCHITECTURAL SUBJECTS

Favourite buildings in your locality, famous buildings here or abroad, can all be celebrated in stained glass.

The architectural studies shown in Figs. 23 and 24 are two stages in the delineation of the old and new Westminster Hospital, part of the window described in the previous subject. Fig. 24 is just a little smaller than the actual size of the work. The tracing stage has been completed. The first elements which were traced were all the uprights, and the perspectives governing the buildings. When all the large shapes are correct, then the detail can be added. Note that the windows of the old hospital and the oriels over the porch are painted a solid black, then the frames picked out with a needle to

give a crisp effect. However, all the lines on the modern hospital are traced. Note the different densities of pigment on the balcony and window outlines: this helps the whole structure to appear as a coherent pattern against the light.

The half-toning can be seen in Fig. 23. The buildings are given definition and depth by the use of shadow. Silk-matting has been applied and modified with a scrub and needle. Finally, a light application of stain warms the features of the garden in the modern hospital and the foreground of the old buildings. Stain adds a decorative element to the pigment, and its colour helps relate the panel to the colours in the overall design: the ruby background of the hospital's panel, the green palms and rich gold ribbons.

PRESENTING A HISTORICAL SUBJECT

In reproducing a subject from an old print or manuscript, you must reinterpret the lines to make it 'read' as

fig. 24 'Westminster Hospital': trace lines

a glasspainting. With the help of the following commentary, you will be able to interpret a favourite scene from a print or old drawing, helping it to live again, be on view and appreciated afresh.

Fig. 25 illustrates a panel to be on display at the new *Mary Rose* Trust Museum at Portsmouth. If you wish to depict a subject with a great variety of detail, like this one has, you must make a cartoon which distinguishes the different types of line. I worked from the Tudor drawing in the Anthony Rolls, drawing all the details in a way which would make the proper impact when painted on glass. For instance, I made all the arcading a solid black feature, to create a rhythmic pattern along the ship; and I made the lower hull a solid black, too, in order to give balance to the many decorative features. The use of solid black in the masts, the arcading and the hull balances not only the fine details but the major

decorative features of the fluttering pennants and the rigging. It also combats halation, so that the light does not destroy the major outlines of the ship.

When I began tracing, I established all the main outlines with a solid black line. After the shape of the ship and its masts was done, I could then begin to tackle the layers of detail, working from the darkest to the lightest. When the arcading and the solid pigment of the lower hull were accomplished, I then put in the pattern of the cannons all along the ship, the thicker rigging, and the flags. I was anxious not to lose the character of the original painting, which has as its outstanding feature the long fluttering pennants. A varying density of line was called for – see the single pennant on the right. Finally, with the lightest touch, all the little emblems on the flags, the planking and nails, and the spider's web rigging were traced. This mesh of fine lines is not only a decorative feature but helps to control the light. The ship was stained in bands of pale and dark gold, with a pale gold on the pennants. I fired the strong tones of stain in the tracing firing, and

fig. 25 'The Mary Rose' based on the Tudor drawing in the Anthony Rolls, (permission of the Master and Fellows of Magdalene College, Cambridge)

the pale tones had a stain firing of their own at a lower temperature. The inscription is picked out of a solid matt with a quill.

PAINTING A STAINED GLASS FACSIMILE

Nothing gives greater insight into the achievements of the medieval glasspainters than a study of a period subject. Choose your example and analyse the conventions used by the glasspainter, which will be characteristic of the period (for more comments on the conventions of the medieval glasspainters, see p. 108).

'The Prioress'

This study of an early fifteenth-century head was done by the Thomas of Oxford Workshop, east window, Merton College Chapel, Oxford (Fig. 26). This head is characterised by exceptionally fine tracing lines and delicate matting. In the earlier periods the bold, strong traced lines bore a relationship to the leading, but by the early fifteenth century the tracing lines had become much softer, more subtle. This elegant painting style was enhanced by the use of a soft lemon stain, never harsh, and a use of large areas of white glass, painted and stained with details, instead of a predominance of dense colours.

I decided to concentrate on the head and nimbus, set against a dark stipple-matted background, all on one piece of glass. The original has a glazed grey-blue headdress. First I prepared a cartoon, made with the help of photographs and my own observations of the original, using binoculars to see the details. Having established the tracing lines and areas of matting on the cartoon, I began tracing on a piece of 'antique' handmade no. 16 white glass – which has a slightly cold green tinge, and is sensitive to stain. The details of the face – eyes, eyebrows, nose and mouth – were the greatest challenge. In attempting to reproduce the expressiveness of line shown in, for example, the long brushstroke for the eyebrow right down round the nose and nostril, I appreciated the extraordinary level of skill attained by the medieval glasspainters, which I consider to be on a par with the celebrated Chinese and Japanese painters, so known and admired in the West. The control of the brush needed to achieve the fluidity of line in such features shows what mastery was achieved by the finest exponents. When we attempt to reproduce such work, we realise that capturing the essence of these superb examples is like chasing the rainbow ... it is always beyond, but in the effort of trying we raise our skills.

fig. 26 'The Prioress' based on an early fifteenth-century head in the East Window of Merton College Chapel, Oxford (reproduced by permission of the Warden and Fellows)

The convention of showing the eye is typical of its period. There is a strong line underneath the top lid, a black dot for the pupil with an outer line denoting the iris, softened by tone. The careful placing of the iris by the medieval glasspainter was deliberately intended to give the effect of a contemplative gaze. The eye is further emphasised by the curved lines of the upper lid, fine lines swinging out from the lower lid to balance them. Traditionally, eyes are the mirrors of the soul, and this explains the great emphasis given to eyes by this glasspainting school.

After finishing all the fine details, I boldly traced on the lead lines; then the piece was fired.

The half-toning processes demanded equal concentration. I worked out of a subtle matt, which I lightly stippled, further softening the effect by light backpainting, which was used at this period. Delicate matts are applied to the back in crucial areas, to control the light. A photograph inevitably loses some of the subtlety in the half-toning, so you cannot judge the effect of the back-painting in the illustration. A virtuoso use of sticklights is a further characteristic of this period. I have used these down the nose, and a dot on the ball of the nose; on the eyes and over the top of the lip. These must be applied with directness and precision as their correct use greatly adds to the definition of the study.

Finally, the decoration on the nimbus was lightly stained.

A HERALDIC PANEL

The acid-etching technique

The technique of acid-etching is considered an aspect of glasspainting, as it is an essential part of producing a traditional stained glass heraldic panel. Heraldry is an exact language, consisting of multiple symbols acquired by a family through its history. Red motifs on white background, white symbols on blue backgrounds, and so on, all have a specific meaning and must be made by the use of flashed glass. As explained on p. 11, flashed glass is usually a white glass with a thin layer of coloured glass on top. The principle of acid-etching is to remove or modify the coloured layer of the flashed glass by exposing it to hydrofluoric acid, but the coloured areas to be retained must be protected from the acid by masking-out – applying a coating of some kind. Traditionally, this was beeswax; I often use embossing black (no. 541), see Suppliers, p. 117); or transparent Fablon is a useful modern substitute. Hydrofluoric acid is a nineteenth-century etching substance. Before that, as early as the fifteenth century, heraldic symbols were made by abrading the flashed glass – painstakingly wearing away the flashed glass with a suitable tool or abrading agent.

Safety precautions

I cannot emphasise too highly the vital importance of stringent safety measures in every aspect of the handling and use of hydrofluoric acid. The acid can cause serious burns. Small amounts dropped on the skin are pernicious, for they are not apparent at first, but can burn insistently for hours afterwards.

Hydrofluoric acid can be purchased from individual chemists, but you will find that not every chemist in your area will be willing to supply you. It is a responsibility for a chemist to sell this acid to the general public, so explain what you want it for, ask for advice in use and assure him that you understand the safety requirements when using the acid. The acid you can buy is 40 per cent strength, 500ml (17.6fl.oz.) in a polythene container. This must be stored, clearly marked as dangerous, in a safe place, preferably in a locked cupboard reserved for it and the equipment connected with it. Its top must be firmly on, as it gives off obnoxious fumes which will affect the surrounding objects.

When using the acid, it is essential to wear protective overalls, safety glasses and rubber gloves – but don't let these perish: check them carefully for pinpoint holes every time you use them, and store them away from the acid. You need a well-ventilated place in which to work, preferably with an extractor fan; or work in the open air. It is essential to have plenty of water at hand, either a tap or full buckets.

NEVER BREATHE THE FUMES OF THE ACID. A specific protective mask, No. 9906, must be worn (see List of Suppliers).

Equipment for using hydrofluoric acid

Strong polythene trays, buckets, a funnel, a measure, and an acid mop (make your own, see p. 59) are required.

Dilution procedure

Add the acid to the water, never the other way round, because water added to the acid can cause a dangerous reaction with possible boiling and spurting. It is usual to dilute the acid in the ratio of two to four parts of water to one part of acid. The ratio depends on your requirements. Very carefully stir the acid round in the tray after you have poured it into the water from the measure. Use a stick, and wash it straight after use.

Making trials in acid-etching

Before beginning a heraldic subject of your own, make some small trials by cutting up a piece of flashed glass into small rectangles and immersing them into different strengths of acid to see what happens and how long it takes for the flash to be removed. Make notes on these trials to guide you in further experiments.

Dragon School shield (Fig. 28)

The shield in this panel is acid-etched on flashed French blue glass. Fig. 27 shows two stages in the etching process, with 27a showing the masked-out stage. I laid the shield shape over the cartoon and lightly traced the outline of the sun and the dragon. I marked the areas to be retained with an initial, as it is very easy to miss a small piece in the masking-out process. I used embossing black, applying it to all the areas initialled: these were all the areas I wished to keep blue. Masking out must be done evenly and checked for pinholes of light, which must be filled in. Any mistakes in going over the line when masking out can be scraped off when dry.

fig. 27 'Dragon School Heraldic Shield': acid-etching stage: (a) the shield masked out; (b) the shield after two immersions in acid

fig. 28 'Dragon School Heraldic Shield': finished panel with tracing and stain (by permission of the Headmaster and Governors)

The back of the glass has to be protected from the acid: I covered the back and edges with transparent Fablon. Traditionally, hot beeswax was painted on, but the transparent Fablon allows you to see the process of the etching perfectly. You may prefer to cut out your motif(s) in Fablon, but, as my dragon shape was complicated, I used the more traditional method of embossing black as a masking agent.

Fig. 27b shows the shield after the acid-etching process. I have given it two immersions in the acid tray because I required two tones of blue. The background blue behind the main subject is the normal flashed colour; the wings and scales of the dragon are a paler blue.

I made a diluted solution of acid in a tray just a little bigger than the glass shape with the liquid just deep enough to cover the surface. The measure was immediately put in a bucket of water. If you are using buckets of water, change them frequently because otherwise the water becomes a dilute solution of acid. Then,

fig. 29 'Christchurch from Merton Field' (private collection, Oxford): this panel has been photographed with the light coming from the side to show the acid-etched textures

wearing rubber gloves, I put the glass in the tray; then dipped the gloves in water.

After 15 minutes or so the acid begins to bite and forms a sediment on the area where it is working. The affected area begins to cloud and you must carefully wipe the area with a simple mop, made by binding a ball of cotton wool onto a stick with thread. This clears the sediment away, but you must wipe with great care as it is easy to damage the edges of the embossing black, and spoil the outline. If you have disturbed the embossing black, you will see black specks in the solution. You must remove the piece of glass to see what has happened. If it is only a tiny flaw, it can be put back immediately, but if the damage is more serious the glass must be washed and touched up or remasked. When the acid has completed its job, the unmasked area will be white.

To obtain two tones of colour I made a second immersion, masking out everything including those areas already treated, except the wings and scales. I watched these areas very carefully and removed the piece from the acid when I saw the required tint. The flash on hand-made glass is always uneven and must be watched carefully – it is not safe to leave the item in the acid solution without checking it frequently. This panel was then traced in the usual way and stain applied where required. Stain applied to acid-etched blue glass creates beautiful tones of greenish-gold, and I have exploited this in the figure of the dragon, deep on the body and lighter over the wings.

Acid-etching in the hand

If you have only a small area to acid-etch, and you want greater control over the process, you need not immerse the piece in a solution but may hold it in your rubber-gloved hand and use the acid mop to apply the acid. Hold the work at arm's length and have plenty of water ready.

Fig. 29, 'Christchurch from Merton Field', is a panel which demanded eight immersions in the acid tray, with the corresponding remasking, and a considerable amount of work in the hand to get the softer effects around the trees, shrubs and foreground and in the sky. The light has been deliberately shone along the surface of this panel to show the textures made by keeping the original strong blue flashed layer.

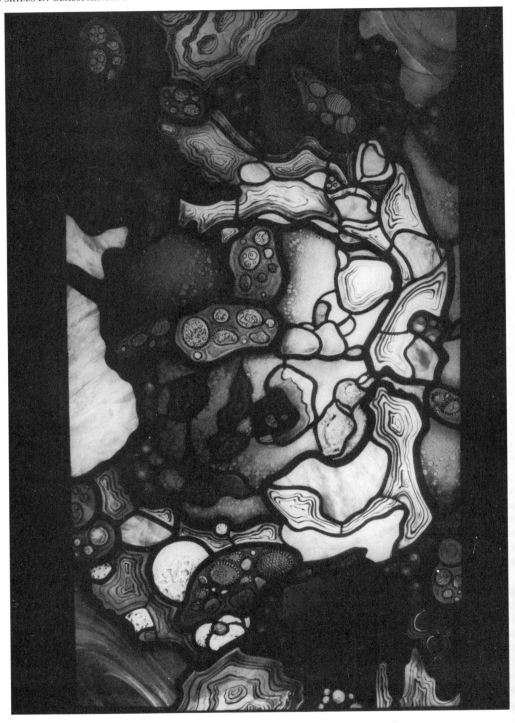

fig. 30 'Inner Space' (also see front jacket): this black and white illustration clearly shows the double-plated acid–etching (globule areas), the water-spotted matts and the use of flexible tracing lines

CHAPTER FIVE

Introduction to the copperfoil technique

ORIGINS AND SCOPE

The copperfoil method of assembling glass pieces is derived from the lampshades made in the USA towards the end of last century and early this century, the best known maker being Tiffany. They were all inspired by the flowing lines of Art Nouveau: their borders were ornamented with swags of fruit, garlands of flowers and swirling foliage. Such shapes required something more delicate than lead calm with which to assemble the many intricate pieces, so a copper or brass chanelling formed from strips of metal was used instead, and the solder applied to it. From this method a copperfoil tape has been evolved to meet the huge hobbyist demand; for from the 1960s onwards Tiffany-style lamps have become very fashionable again. Kits have come onto the market for enthusiasts to assemble; and these lamps are put together by using an adhesive-backed copperfoil, which is pressed onto the edges of the glass and then soldered to hold the structure together. Many other three-dimensional items have been designed for home decoration, all using the same technique.

Chapters 5 and 6 introduce you to a range of items of graded difficulty employing the copperfoil method of construction. As soon as you have made some of these items you will be able to design your own objects. You can make two-dimensional objects such as window panels and 'suncatchers' (the imaginative word used in the USA to describe little window decorations); wallplaques and bordered mirrors. Then there are all kinds of three-dimensional items you can make, ideal gifts, such as plantpot holders, miniature greenhouses (terrariums), vases; lamps and lampshades; boxes, trays, jewellery, mobiles ... In the bibliography (p.116) you will find a list of books containing ideas and patterns for copperfoil items, including Tiffany-type lamps.

REQUIREMENTS (Fig. 31)

Materials

Glass
Usually opalescent or semi-opalescent.

Copperfoil tape
Various widths, according to the specification in the project.

Solder

Flux
Liquid or paste, with flux brush. There is a special paste flux for mirror work.

Masking tape
For three-dimensional items.

Patina
If required, available in copper and black colours.

Tools and sundries

Glasscutter
A standard cutter or a Supercutter, see details of these on p.14.

Pliers
Same as for leaded work, see p.14.

Small pair of scissors
For trimming and cutting foil.

Pointed knife, scalpel type
For removing backing from foil; and trimming.

fig. 31 Materials a[nd] tools: the different widths of copperf[oil] can be seen in the middle; a foiling machine, back left and a grinder, back right. Foiled piece[s] glass can be seen o[n] the right

oo wire wool
For burnishing the solder seams.

Cork
For smoothing down the copperfoil after applying it to the edges of the glass

Wrapped bricks: (or similar heavy rectangular items) for supporting the item at the required angle when soldering.

Glazing nails/workboard
See p. 13.

Soldering iron
Minimum 75 watt, and stand, see p. 14.

Extra equipment (optional)

Foiling machine
There are various foiling machines imported from the USA. If you are going to make many copperfoil items, and need to manufacture them quickly, a foiling machine is very helpful, but it will take time for you to get used to it. Be sure to buy a self-centring one.

Grinder
As copperfoil work depends on accuracy in cutting, a grinder is certainly a great help in cutting the more difficult shapes. It depends on the amount of work you want to do. *Always* wear safety goggles when using a grinder.

MAKING AND CUTTING FROM TEMPLATES

Opalescent and wispy glass is very popular for copper-foil work. You cannot cut (semi) opaque glass using the English method, as descirbed on p. 17 because you cannot see your cutline through such glass. You must make and cut with templates. Or you may prefer to cut on a light table (p. 19).

Making a template

Make two identical cutlines simultaneously: the second will be on thickish card. The layers of material must be in this order: strong tracing paper (e.g. 90g [3.2oz]) on top; then the cartoon; the carbon paper under that; and the card at the bottom. Take a pencil and trace firmly along the centre of all the black lines, pressing evenly to make a clear impression from the carbon onto the card. The pattern you have made on the tracing paper is the cutline for assembling; the pattern on the card is to be cut up into templates.

The pencil line is sufficient indication for copperfoil work. However, for lead work, draw over the pencil line with a felt-tip pen, leaving a 2mm ($\frac{1}{16}$in) line to represent the heart of the lead.

Cutting and using templates

Copperfoil work

Cut up the templates carefully with an ordinary pair of scissors. Place the pieces of card on the cutline: they must be identical to the shapes on the cutline. Cut the glass piece from the template by laying it on the glass and drawing round it with a fine pen; remove the template from the glass then cut *just inside* the black line. It is possible to hold the template steady on the glass and score round it, but the risk of the template slipping a fraction out of position makes the first method I have suggested more reliable. Cutting just inside the line allows for the two widths of copperfoil which will be between the glass pieces when you assemble them.

Leaded work

Cut out the templates with pattern shears. When you cut along the centre of the black line with these scissors, the special blades will cut away a narrow strip equal to the heart of the lead.

Cutting the glass for copperfoil work

The copperfoil technique demands absolute accuracy in glasscutting. The edges must be perfectly even otherwise the pieces will not fit together properly. Read the sections on glasscutting, pp. 17–19.

Copperfoil widths and uses

The following widths of copperfoil tape can be found in this country:

4.7mm ($\frac{3}{16}$in): for 2mm ($\frac{1}{16}$in) glass, e.g. picture glass
5.5mm ($\frac{7}{32}$in): for 3mm ($\frac{1}{8}$in) glass – all machine-made glasses
6.3mm ($\frac{1}{4}$in): for 3mm ($\frac{1}{8}$in) glass, if you need a wider seam
9.5mm ($\frac{3}{8}$in): wider glasses

If your project has no specification, or you are designing your own item, you must consider the strength of the structure and its appearance when deciding on the best width of foil to use. The function of the adhesive-backed tape is to provide a base for the solder. If you use narrow foil on large items, remember that the thin seam may look elegant but will not be so strong as a thicker one. Wider tapes take considerably more solder, so this affects the cost of an item.

Foiling the glass (Diags. 27a, 27b)

All the pieces of glass must be wrapped round their edges with copperfoil. Measure a length of copperfoil round your piece of glass, allowing about 6mm ($\frac{1}{4}$in) extra. Cut this foil off the reel. Place it on a table with the white backing uppermost. You must remove a

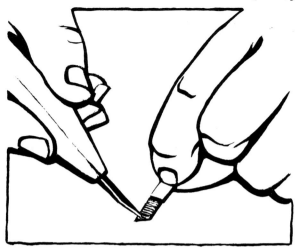

diag. 27a Removing the backing from the copperfoil tape with a sharp instrument

little of this backing so that you can begin to stick the foil to the glass. Take a nail or pointed instrument such as a scalpel-type knife and, holding the foil steady with one hand, pick at the paper backing with the point until a little comes away, revealing the foil underneath. Hold this foil steady with the point of the instrument and gently pull back 6mm ($\frac{1}{4}$in) of the backing. *Don't get over enthusiastic and pull back much or all of the backing, or else the foil will curl and tangle.* Take your piece of glass and lay one edge on the foil with *an equal overlap* of foil on both sides of the glass. Press the glass down firmly on the table so that the foil sticks to the glass edge. Now pick up the piece of glass carefully in

diag. 27b Centring the foil on the edge of the glass

your right hand and, holding down the tape with the third finger, pull the tape backing down little by little. Press the foil to the glass, centring as you go.

There are lots of ways of getting the foil on the glass, but I have found that the method described above is the best way of being able to see that the foil is centred properly. This matters, because if the foil is not centred properly the solder line will be narrower on one side than the other, thus affecting the strength of the item.

Cornering

Continue round the corner about 13mm ($\frac{1}{2}$in), then pinch the foil at the top of the corner between finger and thumb, drawing the overlapping sides to where you first started. After foiling the second side, pinch the foil back to the first corner, and so on, right round the piece to give it a neat finish at every corner. Trim back any excess foil. Using a cork or pencil, smooth down all three edges (see Diag. 28) of foil on your pieces of glass. Don't use a metal object, as it will tear the foil.

ASSEMBLING A TWO-DIMENSIONAL ITEM

Soldering

Lay all foiled pieces on the cutline. If it is a square/rectangular panel, lay the pieces within a right-angle at the left-hand corner of the glazing board and hold in position on the top and right-hand sides with glazing nails. The item must now be tack-soldered – held together at all crucial joins with a blob of solder. Put a dab of flux on a spot to be tacked: tack-solder by holding the hot iron tip to the solder stick just over the place to be soldered until just *one drop* of solder falls down onto the place to be soldered. Hold the iron on the solder blob for a moment. Repeat at all points to be tack-soldered. (See Health & Safety, page 116.)

Now that you have made your item firm, you may solder the seams. Flux one seam at a time. *Always flux before you solder.* Put solder all along the join, then 'run a bead' by drawing the hot iron and solder steadily down a join making a flowing, strong solder line. You will need practice to eliminate bumps and waviness in your seams. *Dont* hold the hot iron too long at any one place: you will crack the glass if you get a heat build-up. Try to avoid breathing the fumes which rise from the flux when you are soldering. These can be avoided if you don't get into the habit of bending too closely over your work.

All soldering must take place with the spot or seam to be soldered in a *horizontal* position. Even a two-dimensional item has an edge which cannot be soldered flat on the table. Stand your piece/panel propped between two heavy objects such as newspaper-

fig. 32 A student gives a final burnishing to her copperfoil technique panel (by courtesy of Oxford College of Further Education)

wrapped bricks and 'pat' solder along the edge. (You cannot run a bead along an edge; only along seams.) I have used the term 'pat soldering' to describe the method of applying solder to the edges of items. This is done by putting the solder stick on the edge and resting the flat side of the iron tip on it for just the time it takes to melt the solder (a few moments), then lifting the iron tip up and placing it down a width of the tip further along and so on in a patting action. If you try to draw the iron tip along the edge in a sideways motion you will merely drag the solder with it. The solder will fall off the edge, leaving too thin a covering on the foil, insufficient to give strength to the edge. It is then likely to tear. Always remember that an edge has three 'sides': a face edge, a top edge and an under edge (see Diag. 28) and all these must be soldered in a horizontal position. Occasionally the edge has to be soldered in the hand because it is curved (such as the edge of the cone-shaped top of the terrarium, Project 12). Wear an old glove on the hand holding the item, for if you get a spot of hot solder on your hand, you will not forget it!

Your aim in soldering a copperfoil item is to get a good even layer of solder on all the seams and edges.

4 Decorative lamps and laminated foil boxes—copperfoil method (relates to Chapter 6)

5 'Supernova'—slumped glass appliqué mirrortile lit with an oilwheel projector (relates to Chapter 9)

6 'Labyrinth' (Project 36, Chapter 9).

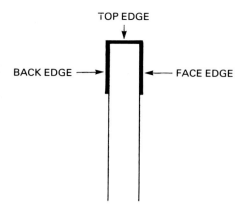

TOP EDGE

BACK EDGE →   ← FACE EDGE

diag. 28 The edge of the glass has three 'sides'

The copperfoil is merely the strip on which to put solder. It has no strength in itself and will soon come apart and/or tear if not enough solder has been applied. If your cutting is not accurate, you will notice that there are gaps in the soldering and when you turn the panel over, the hot solder will seep through to the other side. Patch any considerable gaps with a piece of flat foil, solder, then turn over and patch the reverse side at the same spot before completing the soldering.

PROJECT 9: simple window decoration from glass scraps
Basic: suitable for children

This easy project can be made without involving glass cutting. I have done it with children as young as seven; but they must be very carefully supervised in small groups. I recommend it for Middle Schools.

1 Take 10–15 coloured glass scraps (this is called cullet and can be purchased by the pound from major stained glass suppliers). Arrange the pieces in a cluster on a sheet of white paper on a workboard. The edge of one piece must touch the edge of another piece in at least one place. Children are most inventive and rapidly put the shapes together in attractive patterns, perhaps based on flowers, stars, creatures, vehicles, ships, buildings, letters . . . the possibilities are endless.

2 Carefully pencil round all the shapes, otherwise you will forget the original design.

3 Foil all the pieces, putting each back in its place as you finish it.

4 See the points of contact are pressed together. Dab with flux and solder so that the structure is reasonably firm. Parts of the copperfoil will still show (this is never the case in other copperfoil objects). Carefully turn it over and solder the reverse. Clean gently with a soft dry cloth.

This little decoration has solder only at points of contact so that it is somewhat fragile; but it is a worthwhile simple project as an introduction to glass work. It can be hung by a thin nylon thread looped through a hole in the pattern, or you can solder on a little copper wire hook.

PROJECT 10: geometric hanging window decoration (Diag. 29)
Basic

This is a simple and economical project for beginners and Middle Schools. This panel is based on seven 50mm (2in) squares in three or four colours. I recommend strong, bright colours for richness of effect. If you want to increase the colour combinations, the basic design of seven squares – four kept as squares, two cut in half to form four triangles and the last square cut into four small triangles – can be cut up further.

You can cut up more or all of the four intact squares, turning them into half or quarter square triangles; all this is shown on the reduced cutline. Of course, more smaller shapes means more foil and solder is needed, and the project will take longer. Teachers using this as a classroom project will need to consider these factors.

The panel can be assembled in many ways (Diag. 30), so if a class is making it, each pupil can be encouraged to think out a different combination. For teachers preparing the glass to give their class to assemble, the project can be quickly and economically cut from strips.

diag. 29 Project 10: geometric hanging window decoration – reduced cutline (tack-solder at all places marked O)

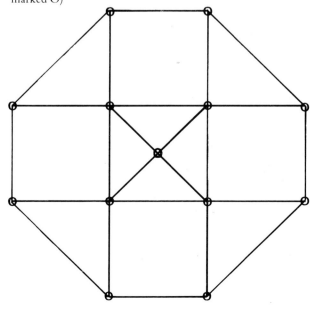

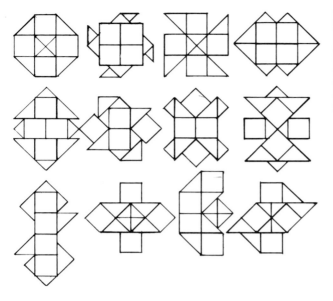

fig. 33 Schoolchildren assembling Project 10 at Pilkington Glass Museum, with the author, 1984 (by courtesy of Pilkington, St Helen's)

diag. 30 Some ways of assembling Project 10

1 Cut all pieces accurately and cleanly (see glasscutting, pp. 17–18).

2 Foil all pieces, paying attention to neat cornering.

3 Lay on a workboard in a pattern you prefer. If your layout contains a right-angle, place this along a straight edge with an object such as a wrapped brick to the left forming a fixed right-angle, and hold the work together with glazing nails.

4 Tack-solder all joins, as circled in the layout shown on the cutline; your layout could be different, according to how you have chosen to assemble your item. There is no need to tack-solder the back.

5 Draw a bead on all seams.

6 Turn over, and solder the reverse.

7 Prop up the panel between two weighted objects and pat the solder along the edges.

8 Fix copper wire hook(s).

9 Clean well.

Designing two-dimensional items

Now that you have grasped the basics of the copperfoil technique, you can design your own little panels/suncatchers. Birds, butterflies, fruit, boats, animals etc. are all popular and pleasing subjects. Remember to keep your shapes simple but well-proportioned. Small items need not be banal if they are well-designed and carefully made, paying attention to finish. I offer you two designs to start you off: Diags. 31 and 32.

ASSEMBLING A THREE-DIMENSIONAL ITEM

Projects 11–13 are three-dimensional objects which can be made after making a basic two-dimensional item. As, in nearly all cases, soldering has to be done with the seam in a *horizontal* position, you will need something to prop your item up with while you construct it. I use bricks wrapped in newspaper (to stop their rough surface snagging the foil); but wooden blocks or weighted boxes will do. Masking tape is used to hold the pieces together, prior to soldering. The good appearance of your item depends on smooth soldering. Your aim is to run a bead along a seam in a continuous action.

When you have finished your item, wash it in warm water with detergent added to remove all dirt and grease. Polish it dry with a soft cloth.

Soldered seams can be left silver: burnish them with 00 grade wire wool. They will need further burnishing from time to time to stay a bright silver. If you prefer a copper appearance, burnish clean with wire wool to get rid of any grease then apply patina. Black patina is also available.

PROJECT 11: plantpot holder (Fig. 34)

This is an eight-sided object which is attractive in opalescent or wispy glass. You could make it in two colours; I have used alternating panels of green and

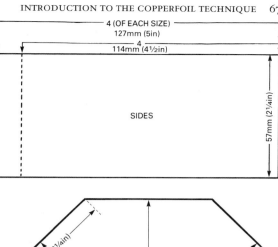

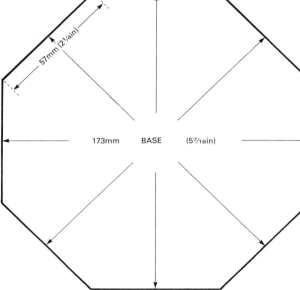

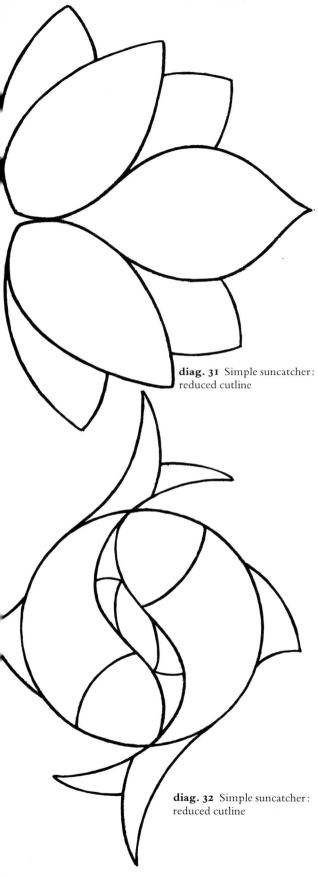

diag. 31 Simple suncatcher: reduced cutline

diag. 33 Plantpot holder: reduced cutline and measurements

diag. 32 Simple suncatcher: reduced cutline

mauve. With careful cutting it can be made from a glass piece 406mm (16in) × 254mm (10in).

1 Enlarge the cutline to the required size: make one template for the side panels. If you want a castellated effect, then cut it down to make the four smaller panels (Diag. 33).

2 If you want an opalescent base, you must cut a template for it. Otherwise use the enlarged cutline and score accordingly.

3 Cut eight side panels and one base, making sure you are accurate. You may choose to include the most interesting parts of the opalescent glass, but the wastage is greater.

4 Foil all pieces with 5.5mm ($\frac{7}{32}$in) tape.

5 Lay the eight pieces of the sides along a straight edge, checking the colour sequence if you are using an alternating colour scheme. Opalescent glass has different patterns on each side: see which side you prefer for

fig. 34 (left) plantpot holder, Project 11; (centre) vase; (right) terrarium, Project 12

diag. 34 Sticking masking tape along the pieces of glass to hold the sides together

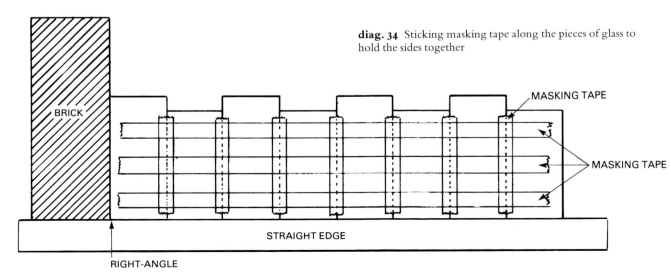

the outside and lay it *face down* on the board. If you are making a castellated item, the bottom of all the pieces must run level along the straight edge.

6 Stick strips of masking tape across all eight panels and down each seam, not quite to the bottom (Diag. 34).

7 Carefully stand the panels up and stand *round* (not on) the base. (If you are making a level-topped item and you find you are a fraction out in the cutting, so that the top is slightly uneven, you can turn the work upside-down after fixing it with masking tape and use the uneven line as the bottom, for you can fill up the gaps with solder. This is not an excuse for bad cutting, but a tip should you find a slight inaccuracy in your sides – it will not do for a discrepancy of more than 1mm.) Fix the two ends of the sides with masking tape.

8 Tack-solder the eight top joins of the side panels; tack-solder the corresponding joins on the inside bottom.

9 Tape all round the inside of the base to prevent any hot solder from falling through should the base not fit perfectly.

10 Carefully pick up the potholder and place it on a side. Solder the base outside edge. Remember you cannot run a bead along an edge: solder by gently patting a layer all along the edge. Solder these outside edges of all eight sides.

11 Turn the pot upside-down and run a bead all round the base seam.

12 Prop the item between two wrapped bricks (or similar) so that a side seam is in a horizontal position. Run a bead down the seam, working from base to top. Do likewise on the other seven seams.

13 Carefully remove the masking tape from inside the potholder.

14 Stand the item on its base and put just sufficient solder on the inside join all round the base. Don't try to solder inside the container with a short piece of solder or you risk burning your hand on the iron. Use a long stick and hold this to the iron tip with your hand *outside* the pot. If you are getting too much solder on the join, melt it and draw the excess towards the centre of the base. Avoid breathing fumes which build up inside the pot. Remember always to wear your mask.

15 Solder all eight inside seams, propping the item in the right position to make the seam horizontal.

16 Pat solder along all outside top edges and inside bottom edges of the sides, turning the container when necessary.

17 Stand on base and solder the top edge to a rounded finish. With a castellated top, solder the sides of the castellated sections in a horizontal position.

18 Clean up and, if desired, apply patina, as described on p.66.

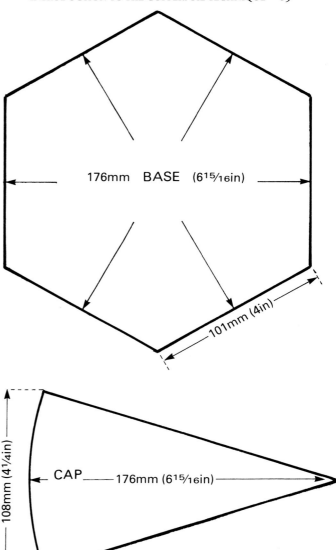

diag. 35 Project 12: terrarium – reduced cutline and measurements

PROJECT 12: terrarium (miniature greenhouse) (Fig. 34)

This six-sided item is constructed on the same principle as Project 11, the plantpot holder. It can be made out of 2 or 3mm glass. The plants need a clear light, so most of the glass must be plain; but one or two sides and up to three panels of the cone-shaped top can be done in a pale coloured glass. Part One is the container; Part Two the conical top which sits on the container. It is therefore very easy to plant and look after your terrarium.

1 Enlarge the cutline to the size you require (Diag. 35).
2 Cut six panels: five at 203mm (8in) × 101mm (4in); one at 193mm (7⅝in) × 101mm (4in). Note that one of them is a little shorter to allow ventilation.
3 Cut the six segments of the top, flattening the points a fraction, as indicated on Diag. 36. Cut the base.

Constructing the container

Follow the steps 4–17 of Project 11, plantpot holder. The method of construction is just the same, except that in the terrarium you have six not eight sides.

Clean up and test for leakage by leaving water in it, standing on some paper. If moisture appears to be seeping, *dry completely* and resolder the bottom joins.

Constructing the conical top

1 Place the six foiled segments of the cone close together, making sure the outside curve is level.
2 Stick a strip of masking tape straight across the top so that it crosses the hole made by the trimmed points. Then stick three strips diagonally from upper right to lower left; three more diagonally from upper left to lower right, and then a strip from top to bottom of every seam (see Diag. 36). This is essential otherwise the cone will lose its shape and not sit properly on the container.
3 Lift up carefully with *the tape inside* and pull round to form the cone shape. Gently press all seams together and tape the two end panels together, also taping the one inside seam where you have joined the cone; then stick two strips of masking tape all round the outside of the cone to maintain its shape.
4 Gently place the cap on the container and check that it sits properly. Put a large blob of solder on the top point, making sure the tape underneath is preventing the solder from dripping through.
5 Check that all the seams of the cone are fitting tightly, then solder the six seams where they are not covered with a band of masking tape. This is one of the rare occasions when you cannot solder in a horizontal position (putting the cone into such a position at this stage would knock it out of shape), so the solder will run down the join. Start from the top and hold the solder stick above the tip of the iron, thus controlling its flow. Then travel down the seam, stopping at the taped areas. Don't worry about the appearance at this stage; it is just to give the joins sufficient strength so that when you remove the masking tape the cone will keep its shape.
6 Remove all masking tape from the outside.
7 Support the cone so that one seam is in a horizontal

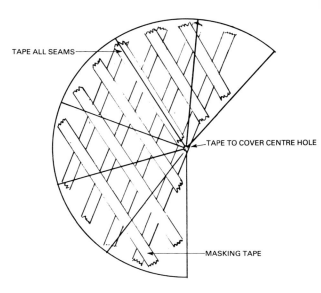

diag. 36 Sticking masking tape to the conical top

position (Fig. 35). Starting from the top, run a bead down to the bottom of each seam.
8 Remove all masking tape from the inside and prop so that an inside seam is horizontal. Draw a bead from top to bottom and repeat on all inside seams. You will need less solder for the inside seams. You can run the bead with the *side* of the iron tip on these narrow seams.
9 Solder all six inside edges of the cone; then all outside edges. Each segment will require repositioning to keep the seams horizontal.
10 Solder the top edge of the cone. As this is curved it is best to solder it in the hand, wearing an old glove for protection.
11 Clean up according to general instructions; apply patina if required to container and top.

Planting a terrarium

Put a layer of small charcoal pieces on the bottom of the container to keep the earth pure. On this place a layer of washed gravel to help with drainage. Above that goes about 76mm (3in) potting compost. Plant two or three bottle plants: remember that they will grow quickly so don't overplant. A terrarium needs a clear light but *not* direct sunlight. Do not place near a radiator. Your terrarium will need the minimum of tending but must be kept damp. Resist the temptation to overwater: spraying once a fortnight with tepid water is usually sufficient. Remove any decaying leaves and trim where necessary.

fig. 35 Constructing the conical terrarium top, propped on supports so that the seam to be soldered is always horizontal

In the diagram labels: TAPE ALL SEAMS, TAPE TO COVER CENTRE HOLE, MASKING TAPE

PROJECT 13: a simple box (Fig. 38)

When you have mastered the construction of this simple box, you can go on to design all kinds of boxes. Opalescent or wispy glass is recommended for this project. If you choose another kind, be sure it is 3mm ($\frac{1}{8}$in) thick.

1 Make a template for the side and the base from Diag. 37. Cut four sides, one base and one lid (the lid is 6mm ($\frac{1}{4}$in) larger overall than the base, less 3mm ($\frac{1}{8}$in) to allow for the hinge). Choose the best parts of your glass, especially for the lid.

2 Foil all pieces.

3 Place a wrapped brick (or similar) at right-angles to the left of a straight edge and lay the four sides in a row, making sure the first fits in the angle and the rest are closely touching. Make sure the side you want on the outside is *face down*.

4 Stick masking tape all along the line of pieces, then a strip down every seam, leaving a gap of 6mm ($\frac{1}{4}$in) at the bottom.

5 Carefully pick up the taped sides and stand *round* the base of the box, with the tape *inside*. Adjust so that the side panels are upright and fitting snugly round the base, then fasten the two ends with masking tape.

6 Tack-solder the top edge join between the first and fourth sides. Repeat on the other three top corner joins.

7 Tack-solder the inside bottom corners to the base. Take care not to use too much solder, because it could cause a crack in the corners. Put masking tape all along the inside seam.

8 Turn the box on its side and pat solder the narrow strip of foil all along the base edge.

9 Turn the box upside-down and run a bead all round the base seams.

10 Decide which is the front of your box, then run a bead along two corner seams, leaving the other two unsoldered where the hinge will fit. These seams must be soldered in a horizontal position, so prop between supports.

11 Remove the masking tape from the inside and solder all inside seams (see Diag. 38a).

12 Put the box on its side and solder the top outside edge and the bottom inside edge.

13 Turn the box the right way up and solder all top edges, making sure you get them smooth and rounded so that the lid will sit properly.

14 Solder the four edges of the lid, remembering that an edge has three 'sides' (see Diag. 28).

Making and fixing the hinge lid

The hinge consists of a short length of brass tubing through which is threaded a copper wire.

1 Place the lid on the box with your favourite side

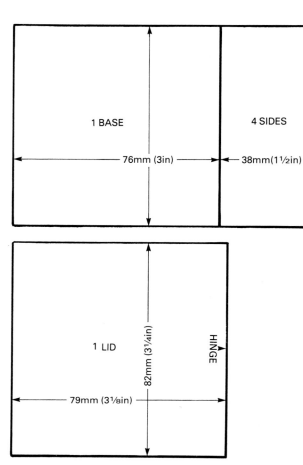

diag. 37 Project 13: simple box – reduced cutline and measurements

diag. 38a Soldering the inside seams in a horizontal position, propped on supports

uppermost. There should be a gap of about 3mm ($\frac{1}{8}$in) at the end to take the hinge.

2 Pick up the box with the lid firmly held in position and bind it with masking tape *parallel* to the hinge to make it secure.

3 Take the hinge (brass tubing with copper wire threaded through it) and make sure that the copper wire protrudes equally at either end of the tubing.

4 Bind these protruding ends of copper wire with masking tape up to where they go into the tubing, to protect them from the solder.

5 Place the hinge in the space at the back of the lid, checking that it is properly centred.

6 Take two small pieces of masking tape and fix the hinge to the lid, leaving room to tack-solder.

7 Tack-solder the hinge to the lid, taking care that you do not solder the lid to the box.

8 Remove the lid, with its tacked hinge, from the box, taking off all the masking tape *except* the two protective pieces on the copper wire.

9 Lay the lid *face upwards* with the hinge flush on the table. Carefully add some more solder to secure the hinge to the lid, then turn it over and solder the underneath. It must not be too thick, however, or the underneath of the lid will not sit neatly on the box.

10 Remove the two protective pieces of masking tape from the copper wire, and clean.

11 Clean the lid and base thoroughly using a cloth dampened with either detergent or methylated spirits.

12 Place the lid on the box with the hinge in position: bind it on with masking tape right round the box *both ways* so that it is absolutely secure.

13 Bend the protruding lengths of copper wire down into position along the two unsoldered seams (see Diag. 38b).

14 Tack-solder the copper wire to the seam, just below the hinge. Unbind the lid to check it works, then rebind the lid to the box and solder the two side seams by drawing a bead. Work carefully from the top; avoid soldering the lid to the box!

15 Clean up.

Designing your own boxes

A decorative lid will give a box a special character. Not only can you make lids which include the shapes of flowers, landscapes, birds, initials etc. in the design, but you can also incorporate semi-precious stones, shells or coins by wrapping their edges with copperfoil and

carefully soldering them into the lid panel. Novel box lids can also be made using the fused glass technique, see Projects 27 and 28 (p.87), and further suggestions, p.92.

Laminated boxes (see colour plate 4)

A laminated box consists of two layers of plain glass with a material sandwiched in between. To learn the basic technique, make a box the same size as Project 13. Use thin plain glass (old photographic plate is ideal), and cut two pieces of all the shapes *except* the base, unless you wish to decorate that as well. Prepare the decorative layer for placing between the two pieces of glass. You must use your imagination to choose this layer. Colour plate 4 shows four boxes using iridescent foils. Other suitable materials are decorative (cut) papers, foiled papers such as Christmas gift wrap, photos, calligraphic poems, attractive fabrics, or plain fabric embroidered with initials or emblems, dried flowers – but these must be as thin as possible. Place your decorative layer between the two layers of plain glass and wrap copperfoil round the shape, treating as one unit. When making this type of box, ensure that the flux does not seep through the foil to the contents – it tends to affect them. For this reason I recommend paste flux for this kind of work, used sparingly.

diag. 38b Pressing the copper wires of the hinge into position down the two back seams

CHAPTER SIX

Advanced projects in copperfoiling

Advanced projects in copperfoiling

All the items in this chapter demand considerable skill: do not attempt them until you have assimilated all the information in Chapter 5, and made it least two projects from it. Read a project through carefully before beginning to make it.

PROJECT 14: Hanging lampshade, or table lamp

This item can be suspended to make a lampshade, or inverted to be an atmospheric table-lamp. In colour plate 4 I have used opalescent glass: the white is a beautiful milky streaked semi-hand-made English opalescent.

1 Decide on your measurements. The units are based on squares with canted corners. Make a mock-up of the item in paper if you want to see what its scale will be when finished (Diag. 39).

2 Decide on your colour scheme for the main shapes, and whether you want to fill the corners in with glass.

3 Cut your glass. If you intend to fill the corners with glass, see instructions after step 11.

4 Foil each square on the two sides which contain the right-angle (see Diag. 39b). This method of foiling the inside seams only, then wrapping the whole unit with an outside foil, gives a continuous surface to the outside seam which will result in better soldering and ease of assembling.

5 Assemble one unit. Be sure it is square by laying it in a right-angle. Tack the central point where the four seams meet, then lightly solder all the seams, beginning 25mm (1in) in from each edge to the centre, making the four pieces one unit.

6 Assemble the other four units in the same way.

7 Wipe the unit clean if necessary, then foil all round the outside. Repeat with all the other units.

8 Make a right-angle with a straight edge and a wrapped brick to the left of it: place the four units along the straight edge, the first snugly in the right-angle, the rest closely touching. Tape with strips of masking tape all along the four units. Tape down each seam.

9 Stand the line of units up and bring sides one and four together to form a square. Tape together to make firm and check the structure is square.

10 You cannot lay the top unit in position because it will fall through. Stick one long strip across the top opening, and another crosswise over it, making a simple cradle. Carefully fit the top, adjusting it so that it sits *on* the edges of the four side units; note, it does *not* fit *inside* (Diag. 39c).

11 Tack solder the structure, starting with the top unit.

Canted corner infills (optional)

I filled in the four top canted corner areas with green glass. If you want to fill in yours, avoid tack-soldering right in the edges of each corner because you need to take an accurate tracing. Place the lamp on one corner and trace through the corner shape from inside, and number it. Write this number on the glass just near this corner. I advise you to make a separate tracing for each corner, just in case the structure is slightly 'out'. Number them all, and the glass.

Cut the pieces, foil them, lay tape across the apertures from the inside so that the pieces cannot fall through, then tack-solder them in position.

Soldering the lamp

12 Carefully remove the masking tape used as the cradle (step 10), but leave the rest till after the outside has been soldered.

13 Run a bead along the cross seams of all five units, from edge to edge.

14 Run a bead along all eight outside seams.

15 If you are leaving the canted corners open, 'pat solder' these edge.

Canted corners
Run a smooth bead along the seams of all four corners.

16 Solder all bottom *outside* edges.

The inside
Remove all masking tape.

17 Solder all the inside seams.

18 Solder all the inside edges.

19 Solder the top edges, holding or propping at an angle so that the soldering is always done on a horizontal plane.

Fitting up the lamp

1 Make four 'eyes' by taking a length of copper wire 76mm (3in), gauge 18; twist in a loop round a glasscutter to form the eye and splay the two ends into a 'T' shape (see Diag. 40a).

2 The hook must be fixed 25mm (1in) from the open end of the lamp, on each of the four side seams. Hold the hook in position with a pair of pliers; tack-solder the nearest end. Then solder the far end; and add more solder to the near end (Diag. 40b).

Hanging lampshade

To suspend from the ceiling, attach four equal lengths of chain.

diag. 39 Project 14: Lamp: (a) Layout of one side (b) cutline of unit (c) how the top fits

Table-lamp

Make a 'spider' to sit in the four 'eyes' (Diag. 40c). See 'Fitting up the lamp' in Project 15 (p.76). Buy a suitable light fitting to put in the 'spider'.

PROJECT 15: table lamp

This advanced item is made up of 16 identically-sized strips of opalescent glass. It is up to you to decide on the size you prefer. With a compass, draw a circle and divide into 16 segments: the width of one segment will determine the width of your strip.

1 Decide on your colour scheme. Illustrated in colour plate 4 is a royal blue and gold opalescent lamp, in alternating colours.

2 Cut 16 strips, choosing your favourite part of the glass for the outside. (Note that the top is cut to fit the cylinder in step 15.)

3 Foil all the pieces.

4 Lay out the 16 strips along a straight edge with a right-angle to the left. Make every alternate strip higher (my lamp has castellation of 19mm ($\frac{3}{4}$in), but you must decide what measurement suits your size best).

5 Stick at least four lines of masking tape all along the row of glass strips; then put masking tape down each seam.

6 With a compass, draw a circle on thick card, the inside diameter of your lamp. Cut out this disc; then make a second identical one.

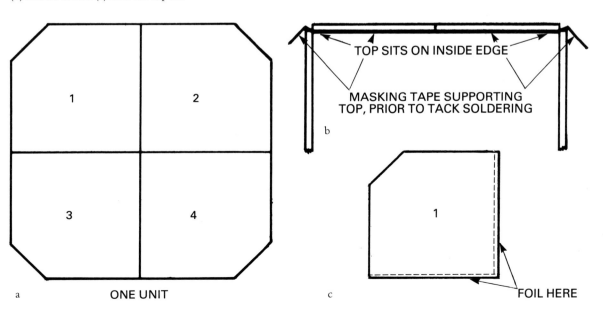

a   ONE UNIT

TOP SITS ON INSIDE EDGE

MASKING TAPE SUPPORTING
TOP, PRIOR TO TACK SOLDERING

b

c   FOIL HERE

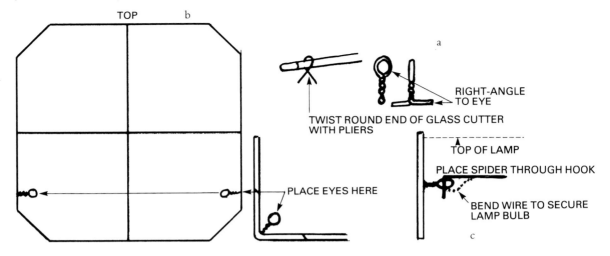

diag. 40 Lamp – how to make 'eyes' and fix them in place
on the lamp

7 Lift the taped strips carefully and place round one of
the discs, fitting so snugly that it holds the disk in place.
Tape securely into a cylindrical shape (Diag. 41).
8 Turn the cylinder upside down with the cardboard
disc in position and carefully push the disc down just
below the castellation.
9 Insert the second disc in position just below the
castellation of the top end of the cylinder. These
cardboard supports ensure that the cylinder shape is
maintained throughout the soldering process.
10 Solder the castellations, top and bottom, as shown
in Diag. 41.
11 Lay the cylinder on its side, supported by wrapped
bricks. Lightly solder every seam from top to bottom,
leaving the castellated areas. This soldering is merely to
make the structure firm.
12 Run a bead down each seam.
13 Remove the two supporting discs from inside, then
take out all the masking tape. Put back one of the discs

to ensure rigidity of the cylinder, and solder the inside
seams. If you have chosen to make quite a long
structure, like mine, you will have to solder from half-
way inside outwards. Remove the support disc and
solder the remaining parts from the other end. Keep
one of the discs for fitting up the lamp.
14 Solder all the edges of the castellation *except* the top
edge, where the top will sit.
15 To make the top, measure the *outside* diameter,
then draw a circle according to this measurement and
make a template. Cut the glass for the top. You can
either use this circle and solder it well so that the shape
is acceptable, or you can go to the trouble of cutting the
16 angles.
16 Adjust the fit of the top and tack-solder into
position.
17 Lightly solder every top edge. Run a bead along
every top seam.
18 Wash and clean up as instructed.

Fitting up the lamp (Fig. 36)

1 Make four 'eyes' as in Project 14 (p.75); solder onto
every fourth seam, 25mm (1in) up from the bottom
castellation.
2 Buy a bayonet fitting bulb holder and a 25 watt
candle bulb.

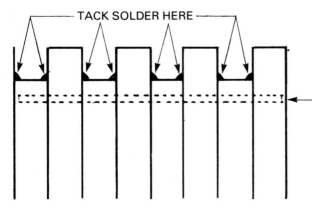

diag. 41 Project 15: where to solder the castellations

3 Make a 'spider': using copper wire, grade 18, wrap the wire round the bayonet fitting to form a ring. Make another ring to fit round the outside of the smaller ring. Solder together to make a solid ring. Take a cardboard disc and place the ring in the centre. Measure the distance from the outside of the ring to the edge of the disc and allow 25mm (1in) extra; then double this measurement. Cut this length of copper wire and bend it in half, pressing the two sides together with pliers. Solder onto the ring. Make three more and solder into position as shown in Fig. 36. Bend the four ends of the spider to make right-angles, as illustrated, so that they sit in the four eyes on the lampshade. Wire up the bayonet fitting and place in the ring. Fit the bulb. Put the spider in position (Diag. 40c).

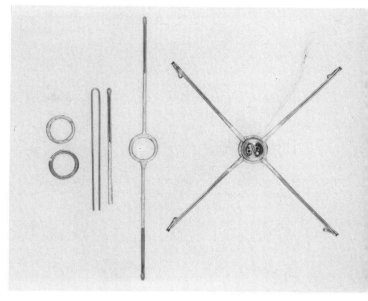

PROJECT 16: yacht mirror (Fig. 37)

This decorative item requires mirrorglass, and this demands special care. Mirrorglass is subject to black spotting along the edges and elsewhere when the mirror backing becomes affected by substances in the flux. I always use the special paste flux manufactured specially to overcome this problem; but I also take the added precaution against damage to the mirror backing by sticking a layer of transparent Fablon over the back of the mirrorglass, extending over the edges and onto the front of the glass. This is then covered by the copperfoil, which both hides the edges and keeps the Fablon in position.

1 Make templates from instructions on reduced cut-line (Diag. 42).

2 Cut both sails, mirror side up. Treat with Fablon.

3 Cut opalescent glass boat and sea.

4 Cut flag. The message of flag A in boating language is 'I want to communicate with you'; flag B says: 'Man overboard!'

5 Foil the sails with 6.3mm ($\frac{1}{4}$in) foil. Do not centre it, but have a narrow overhang on the mirrorglass side and a generous amount on the back. This is so that the structural strengthener of the steel rod can be strongly attached to the back.

6 Foil all other pieces, centring as normal, with 4.7mm ($\frac{3}{16}$in) foil.

7 Assemble the boat-sea area, treating it as a flat panel. Tack-solder, then solder it. Note that the boat has a false seam along its side, for decoration. Lay a strip of 4.7mm ($\frac{3}{16}$in) foil along the boat (see Fig. 37), press it firmly to the glass and solder all along it.

fig. 36 How to make a 'spider' fitting for a lamp bulb and bayonet

fig. 37 Project 16: yacht mirror

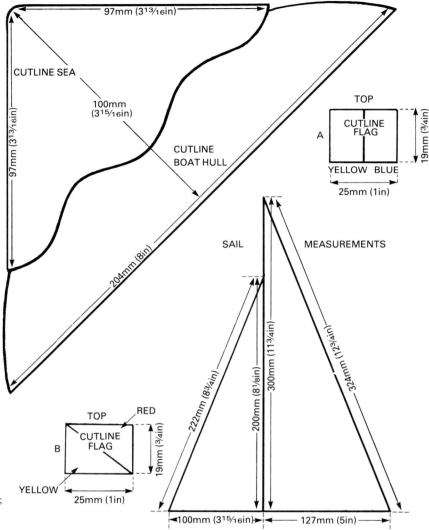

diag. 42 Yacht mirror: reduced cutline for sea/boat hull; two flags; measurements

8 Prepare the longest steel rod by binding copperfoil all along it. If you don't do that you will find it very difficult to solder the rod straight onto the foil of the mirror because, unless the steel is perfectly clean, the solder will keep coming off.

9 Following Diag. 43: place the boat-sea piece face down on the table and lay the large mirror-sail face down in position above it with a 4.7mm ($\frac{3}{16}$in) gap in between the piece and the bottom line of the sail. Then put the bound rod in place: note that it is a little to the left of the boat base, runs up the height of the large sail and protrudes about 50mm (2in).

10 Tack-solder where indicated by circles on the diagram, and all along the mainsail. Then solder firmly.

11 Bind the short rod with foil, then lay in position along the base of the large sail, as shown in Diag. 43a.

Tack-solder, then solder firmly in place.

12 Lay the small sail in position. Solder where it touches the boat at the right-hand end, and at the centre point (circled in Diag. 43a).

13 Measure then place a short length of copper wire from the top of the small sail to the rod of the large sail; solder in position (Diag. 43c).

14 Solder the flag of your choice into one piece, then solder into position at the top of the mast (Diag. 43b).

15 Measure, then solder into position a long length of copper wire from the top of the rod (mast) to the right-hand tip of the boat (see Fig. 37). Note that this is soldered on the front of the object.

16 Affix a copper wire hook on the back (see Diag. 43b).

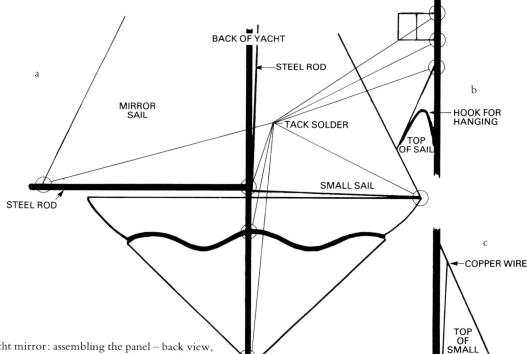

a

MIRROR
SAIL

BACK OF YACHT

STEEL ROD

TACK SOLDER

b

HOOK FOR
HANGING

TOP
OF SAIL

SMALL SAIL

STEEL ROD

c

COPPER WIRE

TOP
OF
SMALL
SAIL

diag. 43 Yacht mirror: assembling the panel – back view, details

PROJECT 17: decorative vase

My vase is carried out with mirrorglass petals and leaves, yellow opalescent centres, and a background of pale blue opalescent glass. The vase is not guaranteed watertight: I have dried flowers in mine, but you can use a liner if you want fresh flowers in it. The cutline (Diag. 44) of one side contains 14 pieces. As there are four sides to the vase, the cutline is used four times, but twice it is reversed (handed). Make the cutline on tracing paper so that you can turn it over.

1 Make accurate templates from the cutline. Write 'a' on every piece; turn over and put 'b'. This will prevent you getting confused over the reversed pieces.

2 Decide on your colours, and use the streaks in the glass to their best effect. Cut all pieces. It is quicker to cut four of each piece, remembering to reverse the template for two of the pieces. Cut the base 76mm (3in) square.

3 I advise you to treat all mirrorglass pieces with transparent Fablon, as explained on p.77. Also, be sure to use special mirrorglass paste flux.

4 Foil all pieces with 5.5mm ($\frac{7}{32}$in) foil, but, as I do not recommend 'double foiling', *leave* all the parts which run along the edge (see Diag. 44). The outer edge foil will be applied after the pieces have been assembled to make on unit.

5 Assemble one panel (side). It is essential that this unit

be made square, with all the edges straight, otherwise the vase cannot be constructed properly. Place your cutline face down on the glazing board then nail a lath along the bottom line. Make a right-angle at the bottom left-hand corner by nailing another lath into position. Assemble the pieces *face down* then nail another lath along the right-hand side of the cutline. Check that the right-angles are true. If you are using 2mm ($\frac{1}{16}$in) mirrorglass (easier to cut than 3mm [$\frac{1}{8}$in]), as it is 1mm ($\frac{1}{32}$in) thinner than the coloured glass, it will sit a little lower than the other glass.

6 Tack-solder *only*: but the unit must be firm enough to handle.

7 Carefully slide out the unit from its laths, and wrap a 6mm ($\frac{1}{4}$in) foil all round the outside edge: this wider foil is needed to supply strength to the structure when soldered.

8 Solder the back but *not* the edges or the front.

9 Repeat the process with the second panel, using the laths in position to guarantee that it will be identical.

10 Remove the laths, turn the cutline over, and make two identical panels.

11 Wipe the panels with a dry, clean cloth then lay all four face down in a row along a straight edge. The left-hand panel must be snugly in a right-angle. Stick lines of masking tape along their length; then a strip down each seam.

12 From now on the basic assembling process is the

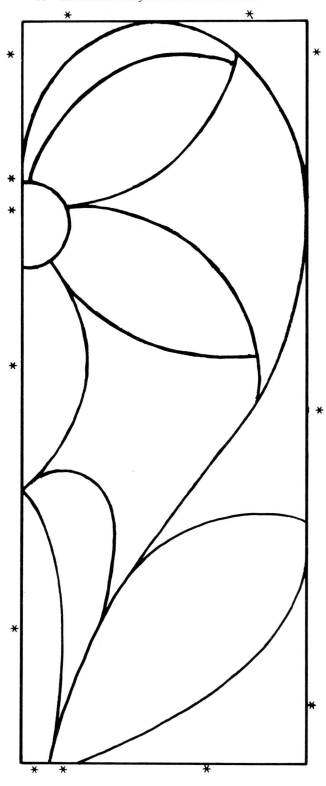

same as for the plantpot holder (p.69ff). Check those instructions as well as the outline which follows here; but you cannot tape inside the base of your vase as it is too narrow.

13 Stand the taped sides up and wrap them around the base; tape the ends together to form a rectangle.

14 Tack-solder the top four corner joins and the bottom inside corners to secure the base.

15 'Pat solder' the bottom four edges.

16 Turn the vase upside down and run a bead along all four seams of the outside base.

17 Solder each panel face as uniformly as possible. The good appearance of your vase depends on your skilled soldering at this stage.

18 Run a bead down each corner seam.

19 Remove all the tape from the inside and solder all four corner seams. Use a long stick of solder with one hand outside the narrow vase shape.

20 'Pat solder' all the top edges.

21 Clean up carefully.

PROJECT 18: waterlily wall plaque

The design for this project appears in Project 6 (pp. 31–2). It would benefit from being spotlit on a wall.

1 Enlarge the design to form a working cartoon in the size you require.

2 Make a cutline from the cartoon. You can make the whole square into a wall plaque, or choose to select just the central subject, as I have done.

3 Decide on your coloured glass. This subject allows you to exploit the full beauty of streaky opalescent glass. I have used Bullseye 'catspaw' opalescent, all the petals cut from one sheet, but the paler tones from one side and the darker, slightly textured colour from the other side. The underneath of a lily pad can be reddish in nature, so I have taken the opportunity to introduce a rich red here, in contrast to the large areas of green. Make best use of the streaks in your green glass to give maximum interest to the colour of the leaves. It is a more expensive way of cutting, to select only the choicest parts of a sheet, but you will be pleased with the results, and the left-over parts can be saved for some other project.

4 I suggest a decorative centre of 37 small pieces, a design demanding skill in cutting and soldering, but giving a filigree effect to the centre of the flower. You may prefer to design a simpler centre. I have used

diag. 44 Project 17: decorative vase – cutline for one side (do not foil outside edges of pieces marked ★ until assembled to make on unit)

fig. 38 Decorative boxes and vases: see Project 17, back row, second from left

mirrorglass for the outer shapes, lemon opalescent for the circles, and an inner ring of radials in iridescent white. Mirror or laminated foil can be used for the three pieces indicating water.

5 Cut all your glass. Note that the shapes of all the petals are slightly different. These are more trouble to cut than a series of identical ones, but I wanted the flower to have a graceful, non-stereotyped appearance. Number each piece as you cut it and put the same number in its respective place on the cutline. This will prevent you becoming confused at the glazing stage. When cutting opalescent either make templates (p. 62) or use a light-table (p. 19). Take extra care to be accurate when cutting the small pieces of the flower centre.

6 The panel will look more pleasing if you use different widths of foil. I have used 4.7mm ($\frac{3}{16}$in) for

the centre and the first ring of petals; 5.5mm ($\frac{7}{32}$in) for all the petals of the next ring; 6.3mm ($\frac{1}{4}$in) on outside petals where they meet the leaves, and 6.3mm ($\frac{1}{4}$in) round lily pads. Careful study of the back jacket will show that I have also graded the types of foil on the leaf veins. Foil all pieces.

7 Tack-solder the central section, held together with pins on flat polystyrene. Tack-solder *all* the pieces together on a glazing board, held by pins. Solder the front; turn over and solder the back.

8 Solder two small copper wire hooks on the back and thread nylon on them to hang on the wall.

9 I have applied black patina to the lily pads, and burnished the silver solder of the flower. This has had the effect of drawing the eye to the flower.

10 For extra interest, I have appliqued little water-drops to the leaves. These are made by heating fragments of clear dalle-de-verre glass to make them smooth (see p. 102). They are then struck to the pad with a rapid-acting super epoxy.

CHAPTER SEVEN

Glass appliqué

This is a bold modern technique, made possible by the development of epoxy resin which is used to stick the coloured glass pieces to the base glass. As it is relatively simple, it is particularly suitable for Middle and Upper Schools: striking panels can be made without glass cutting. In it you can use up all the glass scraps you have over from other projects. Attractive panels can be made without filling in the areas between the pieces of coloured glass with a black grouting substance (see Fig. 39); but the addition of a black background gives the colour richness.

Materials required

Base glass
Use 3mm ($\frac{1}{8}$in) for small panels, but large projects require thicker glass. If you are a teacher ordering a number of panels for pupils, your glass merchant will cut the required sizes for you.

Coloured glass scraps (cullet)
Buy several pounds of this for a good variety of colours, types and sizes. If you have got some opalescent and mirrorglass scraps, these can be used too.

Grouting substance
This is made from a very fine silver sand from a builders' merchants; cement fondu from an artists' materials supplier; and pva adhesive.

Epoxy resin
Use rapid-setting super epoxy, which cures in about ten minutes. (I do *not* advise the instant-bonding glue.)

Frame
If you wish to hang the panel up instead of leaning it on a window ledge, you can frame it with a strip of lead (63mm ($\frac{1}{4}$in) × 6.3mm ($\frac{1}{4}$in) heart). You will need a little solder to join the lead and to fix copper wire hooks. You might prefer to frame it in wood.

PROJECT 19: free mosaic panel (Diag. 45)
Basic: suitable for Middle Schools

1 Prepare the base glass: 200mm (8in) square is big enough for a beginner's panel. Blunt the edges of the glass. Groze the four corners with pliers so that they are rounded: you will be able to frame the panel in lead without having to make mitres.
2 Put a sheet of white paper on the table, place the base glass on it and draw round it.
3 Sort through the cullet and pick out a variety of colours, shapes and, if available, textures of glass. Opalescent and mirrorglass fragments may also be included, but don't use too much of these as they will detract from the transparent glass.

Arrange all these pieces in a pleasing abstract pattern, leaving a 12mm ($\frac{1}{2}$in) border. Take notice of the spaces in between the coloured glass pieces. These will be filled in with a black grouting and so must be considered as part of the design. Don't make the black areas too large in relation to the coloured areas.
4 When you are satisfied with your layout, draw round each piece so that you will know where each piece belongs in your design, removing the pieces one at a time and laying them out elsewhere on your table in about the same pattern as the design.
5 Clean your base glass thoroughly and lay it on the design you have drawn on the paper.
6 With this to guide you, stick your first piece of coloured glass onto the base glass; if both coloured glass and base glass are perfectly level, you can spread a thin layer of glue on the back of the coloured glass and gently press it down so that the resin seeps out at the edges. However, if your cullet contains hand-made

glass, this is uneven, so just put a dab in each corner and stick down, otherwise it will look messy. Use a rapid-setting glue, a type that cures in five to ten minutes: but only mix up the amount you can use in that time, or else your project will turn out expensive. The advantage of the quick-setting glue is that you can go on to the grouting process immediately. For schools, if a class has to finish half-way through this process, the work can be safely stored without the pieces moving out of position.

7 Mix up the grouting by thoroughly mixing two parts of fine silver sand to one part cement fondu. Add a small amount of pva adhesive, stirring with a stick. You need to make it into a dough-like consistency. It must not be runny; nor too dry, or it will crumble. Test a little by picking up a·small amount. You should be able to roll it into a ball without it sticking to your fingers.

8 Take a small amount and pat it onto the base glass between the coloured pieces, using your fingers. Fill the empty areas to just below the surface of the coloured glass. Don't push the grouting down so hard that it creeps under the coloured glass pieces. Avoid as far as possible getting the grouting on the surface of the coloured pieces. Wipe them with a *slightly* damp cloth as you work – clean up as you go along. Don't be tempted to use any water in the cleaning-up process as, if water gets under the glass, it will leave a watermark. As you grout near the edges of the base glass, gently taper it so that the (lead) frame will fit neatly over it. Keep the cut edge clean. Hold the panel up to the light frequently to check that there are no chinks of light. Work on a light-box if you have one.

This grouting process can be left half-way through if you haven't time to finish it, provided that you have cleaned up the surface of the coloured glass in the grouted areas. There is a tendency for the grouting substance to build up on your fingers, so wash them as often as necessary otherwise the stuff on your hands will pull off the amounts already put in place.

diag. 45 Project 19: free mosaic panel – no glasscutting

fig. 39 'Dragon' appliqué panel, done by ten-year-olds (courtesy of Dragon School, Oxford)

Framing the panel

Let the panel set for 24 hours. Measure one side of the panel, multiply it by four then add on a little. Cut this length of lead and stretch and dress it (see p. 20). Wrap the lead tightly round the sides of the panel so that there is no slack. It is best to make the join half-way along the bottom of the panel. Solder it and affix hooks (p. 25).

PROJECT 20: panel, designed shapes from cullet

Basic, see Fig. 39

This project uses the same construction methods as Project 19, but is more disciplined. Sort through the cullet boxes to see what shapes you can find, and what they suggest to you. Then set out your pieces on white paper according to your subject: your name, a flower, a bird, a train, boat, bus, a lighthouse, a monster, a face … all these subjects have been made by my students without having to cut any glass. Your panel can be stuck onto base glass and grounted if you prefer. If you are not grouting, stick your pieces very close together to get maximum effect.

diag. 47 Project 22: 'Butterfly' – reduced cartoon/cutline

diag. 46 Project 21: 'Sunflower' – reduced cartoon/cutline

The following projects involve glasscutting.

PROJECT 21: 'Sunflower' (Diag. 46)

1 Choose your colours: it is economical to cut out of scraps. Each shape can be made up of a mosaic of smaller pieces of similar tone.
2 Using the working drawing as a cutline, cut a number of the shapes then place the base glass on the working drawing and stick on the pieces of coloured glass with Plasticine. Put a little on your thumb and, with the underside of the glass facing you, draw your thumb down the edge of the glass, depositing a small amount all along the edge. Press the piece onto the base glass to make it adhere. In this way you can judge the colour effect as you build up your panel.
3 When you are satisfied with the colour effect in your panel you can begin to stick the pieces to the base glass. There is no need to take them all off the base glass. Remove a small number of them, thoroughly clean them of Plasticine and carefully wipe the base glass, then glue them into position with rapid-setting epoxy resin. Work systematically through all the pieces until you have stuck them all.
4 Grout and frame.

The following projects can be made using instructions from Project 21.

PROJECT 22: 'Butterfly' (Diag. 47)
Window panel or wall decoration

The long shapes of the butterfly's wings look attractive if made up of smaller shapes of slightly different tones. This panel could be made out of opalescent glass and mirrorglass and used as a wall plaque.

PROJECT 23: Magdalen Tower, Oxford (Diag. 48)

A variety of smaller shapes demand skill in cutting. Remember to keep your cutting reasonably accurate, as it is the coloured shape which is read by the eye, not the black grouted areas. This panel looks attractive in tones of one colour.

diag. 49 Project 24: 'Medieval Grotesque', – reduced cartoon/cutline

diag. 48 Project 23: 'Magdalen Tower, Oxford' – reduced cartoon/cutline

PROJECT 24: 'Medieval Grotesque'
(Diag. 49, Fig. 40)

This creature is based on an outside boss on New College Chapel, Oxford. There are some difficult shapes to cut. Pay special attention to the whiskers and the eyes. You can use some startling colour contrasts to bring out the strangeness of this monster. My illustrated panel has red hair and whiskers; red and yellow eyes; purple under the eyes; bright green and blue-green face; and a yellow background.

PROJECT 25: candleholder (see Diag. 50)

This project involves the application of glass appliqué to three-dimensional items.
1 Cut four base glass rectangles 203mm (8in) high × 178mm (7in) wide (or the size you prefer); and a base glass 178mm (7in) square for the bottom.
2 Work out a free mosaic or a design to be cut.
3 Appliqué the four sides and fill in the areas between the coloured glass pieces with grouting, as described in Project 19. Pay special attention to the tapering of the grouting near the edges of the base glass.
4 When the grouting is set hard, wrap copperfoil round all the panels and the bottom panel and assemble according to the instructions for a three-dimensional item in Chapter 5 (p.66).

diag. 50 Project 25:
candleholder – design
suggestion

fig. 40 'Medieval
Grotesque': finished
appliqué panel

FURTHER IDEAS FOR GLASS APPLIQUÉ

1 Make up a number of fused glass simple motifs based on methods described in Projects 26, 27 and 28, and use them in a glass appliqué panel or three-dimensional item.

2 Design pieces of glass with glasspainting and staining subjects on them, either abstract patterns or simple traced subjects such as birds, or leaf outlines. Make these then incorporate them in a glass appliqué panel or three-dimensional item.

CHAPTER EIGHT

Fused glass

Fused glass is glass which has been heated at a sufficiently high temperature for it to melt into its base glass or other pieces of similar glass nearby. The essential requirement is the use of glasses which are homogenous; because if glasses of different types are heated, when they cool they will crack and maze in many places as tension develops between the different constituents.

As the streaky rolled cathedral glass I used for this chapter's projects is no longer manufactured, I suggest using American glass from Bullseye Glass Company. Opalescents, cathedral and two-colour mixes are available. Spray A Overglaze (clear, low-melting ground glass suspended in a spray medium) is recommended to prevent the devitrification of the glass surface during cooling; it should be sprayed over the fused project before firing. Remember to wear your mask. To use your kiln economically, make several trials from Projects 26, 27 and 28 in the same firing.

PROJECT 26: simple shapes (Fig. 41)
Basic: no glasscutting

Take a few scraps of Bullseye cathedral glass, of mixed colours, and experiment with laying them on top of each other, or just overlapping. Take care when using reds because this colour tends to increase in density when fired and may upset the balance of colours. If you want a clear red you can lay other colours out so that there is a gap in the layout; then place your red over the gap and its bright colour will be retained. Transfer your project onto a prepared batt.

Preparing the batt

When firing at a fusing temperature, over 700°C (1292°F), I take the added precaution of painting battwash onto the kiln batt (shelf). Battwash is used in pottery to prevent glazes sticking to the kiln furniture and can be purchased from any pottery suppliers. I then place a thin layer of 'dead' plaster (see p.39) on top, to be doubly sure. If you want the back of your glass to be smooth, lay a newspaper on the plaster and smooth it over with your hand, but if you prefer a more textured back, leave the plaster after you have sieved it on.

PROJECT 27: simple shapes on a base glass
Basic

Cut a base glass rectangle, 90mm (3½in) × 75mm (3in) using clear cathedral glass. Lay a number of scraps of coloured cathedral glass on the base glass in a pattern which pleases you. You can secure the pieces to the base glass with a weak solution of gum arabic painted on their undersides to stop them slipping as you take them to the kiln on the prepared batt.

PROJECT 28: designed and cut shapes on a base glass
Basic

Look at Figure 41 (bottom left). This is made up of a turquoise mountain shape; a royal blue suncircle; two strips of yellow; and a mulberry/yellow striped cloud. Design a simple theme for your base (same size as in Project 27), cut the glass pieces and lay them out according to instructions in Projects 26 and 27.

Firing simple fused glass projects in the kiln

The kilns I have recommended for glasspainting are also suitable for fusing (see p.38). Small pottery kilns are also suitable; but obviously it is not economical to fire small projects in a large chamber.

Place your projects on the prepared batt in the kiln and close the door. Turn the kiln on to 750°C (1382°F). Cathedral glass will fuse between about 700 to 750°C (1292–1382°F), according to the kiln (see my remarks on the problems of firing,

diag. 51 Key to Fig. 41

fig. 41 Fused glass projects: (top) Project 26, 1 and 4; pieces for mobiles, 2 and 3; (middle) Project 27, 5 and 6; (bottom) Project 28, 7; Project 31, 8

p.42). If your kiln has a spy-hole, look through it frequently as the temperature approaches 700°C (1292°F). Otherwise you must peep through the slightly-opened kiln door but, as with an oven, beware the blast of heat. You will see the glass melting: it is cherry red, the edges soften and the pieces begin to fuse. It is up to you how far you want a melted effect. It can be more interesting if the edges are not melted too much. Your aim is to turn off the kiln *just before* the optimum temperature, because the heat will continue to increase for a little, even after you have turned the kiln off. You must allow for this; and you will only learn from experience. Leave the pieces to cool in the kiln for 18–24 hours. Don't be tempted to take them out too soon, as the drop in temperature will cause them to crack. All kilns have peculiarities: some places

in the chamber are hotter than others – you must experiment to get to know these places, and fire accordingly. Experiment with several batches of Projects 26–28 before embarking on larger projects.

Displaying items based on Projects 26–28

I assume that the first batches of Projects 26–28 are just to gain experience. Examples of Project 26 can be used in Project 35. Examples of Projects 27 and 28 can be used as box lids or stood on window sills. But if you want to hang examples, you can put hooks on Project 26 pieces by following the instructions in Project 29, step three. The rectangles of Projects 27 and 28 can be edged with copperfoil, soldered, and copper wire hooks added (see Project 10).

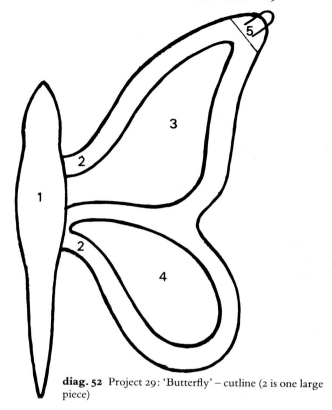

diag. 52 Project 29: 'Butterfly' – cutline (2 is one large piece)

fig. 42 Projects 29 and 30: a mixture of butterflies, flowerheads and a sunflower hanging in a window

PROJECT 29: 'Butterfly' (Diag. 52)

Basic

This butterfly consists of two white base glass shapes, one handed (reversed); four coloured shapes (two handed); and a body of dark brown glass.

1 Cut the glass shapes.

2 Place on a prepared batt, see Fig. 43 (left).

3 Make two little nichrome wire hooks. Lay one on top of each wing tip and cover with a small piece of plain glass the same shape as the wing tip (see Diag. 53b). When these little pieces melt, they will fasten the hook to the wing.

4 Fire at 700–750°C (1292–1382°F). Allow to cool.

PROJECT 30: 'Flowerhead' (Diag. 53)

This flowerhead consists of one petal cut 16 times. You can use white base glass for eight of the petals, alternating with colour(s) of cathedral glass. The centre is made of fragmented glass. A variety of these flowerheads appears in Fig. 42.

1 Cut 16 petals according to your colour choice.

2 Lay eight petals to form a ring, on a prepared batt. Try not to disturb the level surface of the plaster too much when laying petals out, for the melted glass will form to whatever unevenness is underneath it. Lay the second ring of eight petals in between the first circle, as shown in Fig. 43.

3 Take some scraps of cathedral glass (various colours or similar tones, as you prefer). Put on safety goggles and, using the cutting edge of a pair of pliers, snip off small irregular pieces into a receptacle such as a plastic cup. Do not use a wide-rimmed container as splinters of glass will fly all over the place. Lay the cup

fig. 43 Projects 29 and 30: 'Butterfly' and 'Flowerhead': (left) on the batt unfired; (right) fired. Note how the hooks fire into the glass.

diag. 53 Project 30: 'Flowerhead' (a) Cutline for petal (b) how to make and fix a hook into the fused object

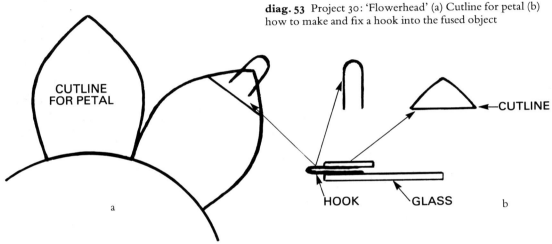

on its side: cutting is done *inside* the cup. Have a newspaper under the cup to catch any stray fragments. Store your snippets of glass according to colour in different containers.

4 Sprinkle your glass fragments into the centre of the flower. If you want a lacy, delicate effect, sprinkle only a thin layer: when the glass melts it will form a mesh of random holes which is attractive. If you prefer a rich, solid effect, sprinkle a thick layer into the centre.

5 Make two nichrome wire hooks; place them in position with little pieces of glass laid on top (see Diag. 53b).

6 Fire at 700–750°C (1292–1382°F). Allow to cool.

Applications of simple fusing

Mobiles

Several small fused glass pieces, made according to the principles explained in Projects 26 and 27 can provide the decorative elements of a mobile. To hang these pieces on the mobile, either affix nichrome wire hooks, as described in Project 29, step 3, or wrap copperfoil round them and solder a copper wire hook to the foiled border (Chapter 5). The mobile pieces can hang from strips of special wire, each suspended by nylon thread.

Christmas tree decorations

Using the same technique as for mobiles, colourful and unusual Christmas tree decorations can be made.

Box lids

If you want an unusual box lid, make one using the technique described in Project 28. Remember that glass can alter a little in the kiln, so you cannot design the size of the box until you have your finished fused glass lid.

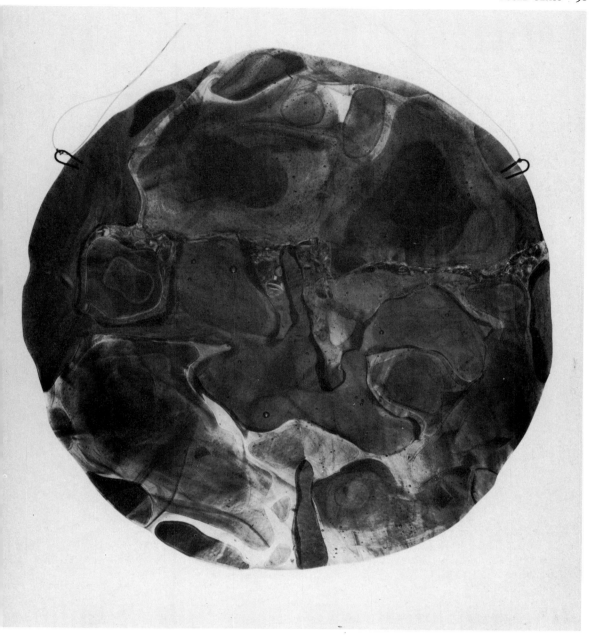

3.44 'Satellite Picture' roundel. Layers of fused glass showing a semi-abstract Southern Europe and North Africa. The colours are bright blues, browns, oranges and greens.

PROJECT 31: combining fused glass and glasspainting

Basic

Make a trial panel on a base glass 110mm ($4\frac{5}{16}$in) × 90mm ($3\frac{1}{2}$in) (see Fig. 41, bottom right).

1 Cut a base of plain white streaky rolled cathedral glass.

2 Trace various lines and patterns on it (see Tracing, pp. 39–41).

3 Lay pieces of coloured cathedral glass on top in an interesting colour and pattern combination.

4 Place on a prepared batt and fire at 700–750°C (1292–1382°F). Allow to cool.

Applications of combining fusing an glasspainting

Combining these two techniques opens up man possibilities. Fig. 45 shows a large traced and fused gla butterfly, of white base glass with rich shades of blu and purple. Designs have been painted on the base gla then overlaid with the colours and highly fired t produce a completely smooth surface. In my kiln this achieved at about 780°C (1436°F). Fig. 46 shows roundel based on an aerial photograph of strip farmin in the USA. This panel is not interpreted naturalistica ly: the strips are done in blue glass, buildings in re The details are traced on before the overlay of colou This panel has been fired at a lower temperature tha the blue butterfly to retain some texture in the laid-o glass pieces.

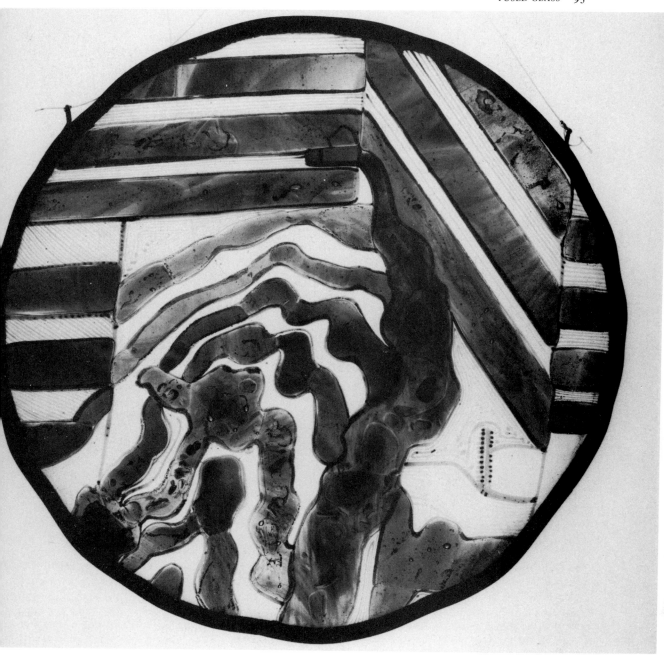

45 'Large Butterfly': traced and fused glass in rich blues,
~ple and white

46 'Aerial Photograph' roundel: based on strip farming
America. Non-naturalistic colours: blues and greens with
~ed details

CHAPTER NINE

Fused glass appliqué and other decorative techniques

All kinds of decorative techniques open up from aspects of fused glass, which can be used for wall and window decoration. The following projects have been developed from my experiments since 1971. Do not attempt these projects (except Project 36) until you have made some of the projects in Chapter 8.

PROJECT 32: 'Harlequin' wall decoration
Basic: Appliquéd softened glass on mirror

Applications of this basic project can lighten dark areas of a hall, corridor etc., especially when lit with (coloured) spotlight(s). This panel is based on a standard 30cm (12in) mirrortile, tinted if you prefer, framed by a ready-made silver frame, which is put on after the tile has been decorated. The decoration consists of 16 triangles of A: 70mm (2$\frac{3}{4}$in); 16 triangles of B: 50mm (just under 2in). You can use plain or pale tinted glass, I suggest four different colours; or four tones of one colour. Your aim is to lightly soften the edges of these cut shapes in the kiln and appliqué them onto the mirror (Diag. 54).

1 Cut your pieces of glass and lay them on a prepared batt. They must not touch. As there are 32 pieces, you will probably have to fire them in batches.
2 Heat the kiln to about 700°C (1292°F), watching for the edges of the glass to soften. You need not fire them beyond that temperature.
3 Allow to cool, remove from batt and wash carefully.
4 Stick the 16 larger triangles onto the cleaned mirrortile, using quick-setting super epoxy (not instant bond). Spread the glue in a thin layer all over the back of the glass, but not so much that it will ooze out at the sides when placed on the mirror. Then appliqué the 16 smaller triangles in the pattern you have chosen.
5 Frame with the ready-made frame or fix onto the wall with mirror fixings.

Applications of this technique

Fig. 47 shows 'Silver Jubilee' (1977) which employ⊢ this technique of cut shapes with softened edges. The four crowns pointing into the corners are in ream⋅ white 'antique' glass, fired hotter so that the glass ha gone slightly milky; the other four crowns are in seed⋅ glass, which glitters in the spotlight. The crowns ar⋅ filled in with crushed glass. The main parts of th⋅ crowns were fused as well as softened round thei⋅ edges, and the 'jewels' appliquéd.

Both abstract and figurative designs can be made i⋅ this technique.

PROJECT 33: fused glass appliqué bordere⋅ mirror
Basic

Mirrors can be made most attractive by sticking o⋅ fused glass borders. They look better if the gla⋅ appliqué forms the border and is not hedged in by ⋅ frame. You can use standard mirrortiles which have ⋅ finish to their edges; or you can cut mirrorglass an⋅ edge it with copperfoil. (Use a special mirrorgla⋅ flux when soldering.) This leaves the problem of th backing, both to give strength and provide som⋅ thing on which to put fixings in order to hang th⋅ mirror. I back mine with hardboard, see steps 6–⋅ The borders are made by fusing fragmented cathedr⋅ glass.

1 Decide on the layout, measurements and colours ⋅ your borders. Two possibilities are shown in Diag. ⋅ An example of unfused and fused fragmented gl⋅ borders in shown in Fig. 48.
2 Prepare the batt and outline the dimensions of yo⋅ borders in the plaster with a sharp point.
3 Prepare amounts of fragmented cathedral glass in t⋅ colour(s) you require, using the method described ⋅ Project 30, step 3.

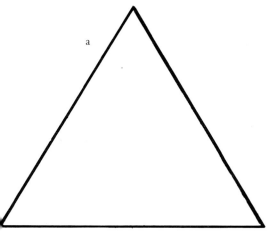

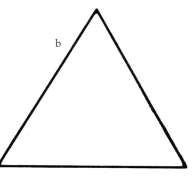

a

b

diag. 54 Project 32: 'Harlequin' wall decoration – cutlines

fig. 47 'Silver Jubilee' appliquéd mirror panel

a

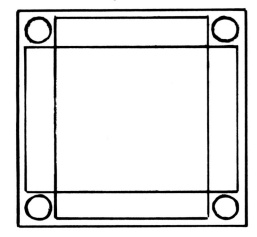

b

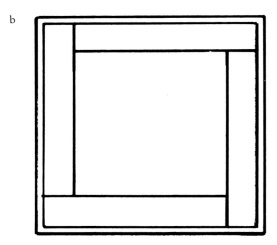

diag. 55 Project 33: two suggestions for layout of mirror borders

fig. 48 Project 33: fused glass appliqué borders: (left) unfired; (right) fired

4 Sprinkle your fragmented glass directly onto the batt within the areas you have outlined in the plaster. A thin layer gives a lacy effect; a thicker layer results in a solid border.

5 Fire the glass at a fusing heat 750–780°C (1382–1436°F). It is up to you how smooth you want your borders to be. Around 750°C (1382°F) the edges of the glass fragments will still be giving a textured effect, but as the kiln temperature rises the surface will become perfectly smooth. Always remember to turn the kiln off *before* you reach your optimum firing temperature. Allow the work to cool for 18–24 hours.

6 Prepare the back of the mirror by cutting a hardboard base the same size. You can stick Fablon baize on the back for a neat finish.

7 Fix two split rings on the back for attaching cord. This can be done by drilling a hole in the places where they are to be fixed and threading a copper wire tie through each one; these ties are then flattened to hold the split rings firm (see Diag. 56). They will not scratch the back of the mirrortile because it has adhesive pads. When you stick the board to the mirrortile, a small gap, 2mm ($\frac{1}{10}$in) exists between the back of the mirror and the hardboard.

8 Remove the fused glass borders from the batt and carefully brush the plaster from them with a soft toothbrush. Wipe with a slightly dampened cloth if necessary.

9 Stick the borders in position on the mirrortile, putting a thin layer of rapid-setting epoxy resin all over the back of the glass shapes.

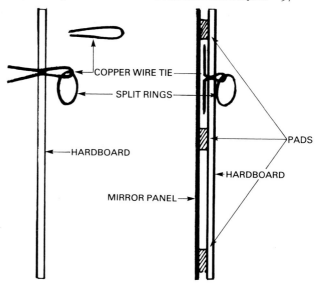

diag. 56 Project 33: mounting the mirror on hardboard; fixing the hook

fig. 49 Fused glass appliqué wall panel

Applications of this technique

You can plan out larger decorative areas on parts or all of a mirror. Fig. 49 shows a decorative mirrortile with a spectrum of fused glass colours appliquéd onto it, textured by a number of 'jewels' made of small pieces of heated dalle-de-verre (for how to make these see Project 35, step 4). These are stuck on the coloured glass after it has been mounted on the mirror. Such decorative items, spotlit, make a focal point in a room or enliven dark areas.

fig. 50 Project 34: slumped glass bordered mirror

PROJECT 34: slumped glass bordered mirror (Fig. 50)

This project involves a lot of work, but when once you have got used to making moulds for slumped glass, you will find you can make fascinating three-dimensional pieces in the technique. This project is based on a standard 23cm (9in) mirrortile. Before you can work with glass you have to make fired clay shapes on which you will place glass strips. When the glass is fired it will sag (slump) over the moulds, taking up the required shapes. These sculptural pieces can then be stuck to mirrorglass.

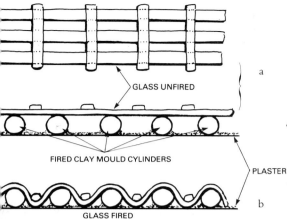

diag. 57 Project 34: (a) layout of glass strips from the top, (below) layout of glass strips on the cylinders, seen in section; (b) fired glass, seen in section

Making the mould shapes

1 Make 20 cylinders of clay, diameter 12mm ($\frac{1}{2}$in), length 76mm (3in). Fire in a pottery kiln at 950–1000°C (1742–1832°F), normal biscuit firing. There is no need to standardise these cylinders, the slight irregularities they cause in the glass shapes is part of the charm of the design.

Making the slumped glass borders

1 Note that the borders consist of four strips of slumped glass and four corner squares. Decide on your colours. I suggest you use cathedral glass decorated with blue chips, and blue glass corners.

2 Cut your glass pieces. Each border contains three strips of (white) glass, 152mm (6in) long × 6mm ($\frac{1}{4}$in) wide; four strips varying between 38mm ($1\frac{1}{4}$in) and 50mm (2in) long × 6mm ($\frac{1}{4}$in) wide. Cut four borders. Cut four corners in the decorating colour of your choice, just under 38mm ($1\frac{1}{2}$in) square. It is best to cut these squares a little on the small side in case the slumped borders spread a little more than expected.

3 Prepare the decorating colour fragments as described in Project 30, step 3.

4 On a prepared batt, place five fired clay mould cylinders in a row along a marked stretch of 152mm

(6in), spaced equally. Paint them thickly with battwash before setting them out on the batt. Then, as an extra precaution against the glass sticking to them, dust on some 'dead' plaster of Paris. Lay three long strips of glass along them, then lay the four varying-length short pieces at right-angles on top of them, one between each cylinder (see Diag. 57a). Dab on a weak solution of gum arabic and sprinkle with decorating coloured fragments. If your batt will take more of the slumped borders, lay them on; otherwise make the others at a second firing.

5 If there is room on the batt, take the four corner squares, dab on gum arabic and scatter the same colour fragments on them to give texture. Place on the batt.

6 Carefully transport the batt to the kiln and fire around 700–750°C (1292–1382°F). Watch the glass as it begins to slump over the moulds but do not over-fire it: it will spread too much. Leave 24 hours to cool completely.

7 Lift the glass borders off the batt. The cylinders should come away fairly easily if you have prepared them properly. If the glass is gripping them, scrape off the battwash and turn the cylinders *very gently* to release them. Clean the glass by brushing with a soft toothbrush, then a slightly damp cloth.

8 Prepare the back of the mirror, see Project 33, steps 6 and 7.

9 Lay out all your cleaned border and corner pieces on the clean mirror and adjust. Fused glass pieces, especially if fired hot, do alter shape in the kiln so you will need to work out a nice adjustment of the borders to the corners. Should you find that a border has slumped unevenly so that it doesn't sit properly on the mirror, it will need supporting with a little piece of plain glass (see Diag. 58). Glue this support to the border before gluing it in position on the mirror. You may need to make several supports on the borders.

10 Stick all pieces with fast-setting super epoxy to the mirrortile.

Further applications of slumped glass

According to the variety of clay mould shapes you make, you can experiment with a great number of slumped shapes. Fig. 51 shows a table decoration 'Dragonfly on lily-pad'. The leaf undulates: this effect has been obtained by making an undulating mould the

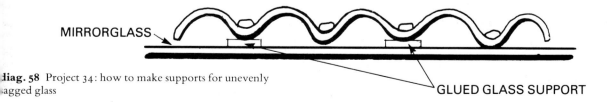

diag. 58 Project 34: how to make supports for unevenly agged glass

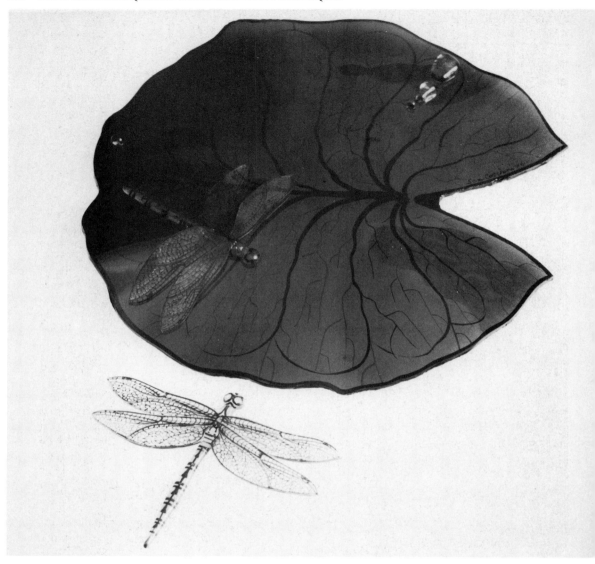

fig.51 'Dragonfly on a Lilypad'

shape of the leaf. The leaf and the dragonfly have been hand-painted (traced) in great detail. Dewdrops made of fragments of dalle-de-verre, heated, have been appliquéd to the leaf.

Fig. 52 shows a much more sculptural piece, made on a series of domed moulds. The reflections create an intriguing visual illusion when mounted on mirror-glass. This piece is lit with coloured oilwheels which give the effect of coloured liquids running through the glass in a continuously-changing pattern. Colour plate 5 gives an idea of the vividness such a work, lit imaginatively, can have. This panel, 'Supernova', has

been laid over cylinder moulds to create an undulating effect. It is made in plain glass with a blue centre. It can be lit with a variety of lighting systems, each bringing out a different aspect of the subject.

PROJECT 35: fused glass appliqué on window panels

In the mid 1970s I developed a series of window panels with the collective name 'Pelagos', because they seemed to me like islands of colour in seas of rippling plain glass. Fig. 53 shows a more complicated version of this type of panel, with fused glass motifs appliquéd onto both sides of the glass, so that it can be turned

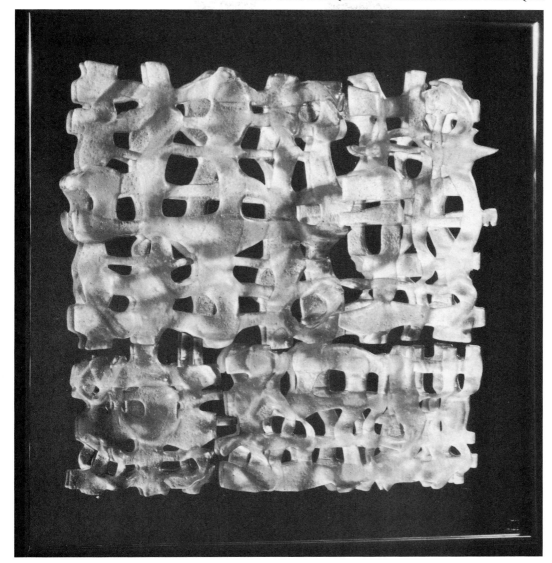

Fig. 52 'La Glace': sculptural fused glass appliqué

ound and viewed on the second side – neither is the 'right' side – it depends on your mood which side you wish to have facing you. The fascination of making this sort of panel is that each one is unique, a combination of fused glass pieces which can never be repeated. The success of such compositions depends on a variety of glass shapes from which to choose. The main motifs are made according to Project 26; the lacier ones use the technique in Project 33, and the single 'jewels' are formed from broken dalle-de-verre. Whenever you are heating the kiln to over 700°C (1292°F) for another project, you can fill the batt with little pieces for this type of panel, building up a store that will inspire you in creating new designs. You can also appliqué items such as vases with these pieces (see Fig. 38).

1 Make a window panel not more than 300mm (11⅘in) using an interesting background glass such as a reamy (the 'antique' is the most beautiful) or a seedy in white or a pale tint. Frame it in lead and affix hooks.

2 Look through your store of fused glass pieces, or make some batches, then select the main shapes and lay them out on your cleaned glass panel.

3 Lacier pieces of glass, which have been made of little pools of fragmented and crushed glass which have been fired, must be placed in pleasing relation to the larger bolder shapes. A pair of tweezers is useful in handling these fragile shapes.

fig. 53 Two-sided 'Pelagos' panel

4 Bold single 'jewels' give the final balance to the composition. Buy a dalle-de-verre slab of glass, wrap it in old cloth and break it into pieces with a lump hammer (wear goggles). The resulting fragments of various sizes can be placed on a prepared batt, heated to around 700°C (1292°F) so that their edges soften, then used to appliqué onto any project, not only window panels and wall decorations but box lids, vases, etc.

5 Stick all pieces of glass onto the panel with rapid-setting super epoxy.

Further applications of fused glass appliqué window panels

When you become more experienced in fusing lar shapes, more ambitious shapes can be undertaken. N largest project in this technique was 'Greek Islan (1980)', twelve back-lit panels based on the outlines Greek islands for a client in Athens (see Fig. 54). As t chamber of my kiln was not large I had to make the in sections and fit them together. These panels we double-glazed to keep the appliquéd shapes clean. the main shapes I stacked four or five tints of colour places to obtain richness and variety of tones. deliberately kept some areas thin so that, when fire little holes appeared; and over these I appliquéd 'jewels' of pure colour. The technique will respond to your inventiveness.

PROJECT 36: opalescent glass picture

Opalescent glass, especially the hand-made sheets available, has the most amazing swirls, streaks, shapes and colours in it. It is a challenge to interpret these markings in whatever way you choose. Colour plate 6 shows my interpretation of a marvellous piece of glass which suggested to me a creature-shape in the centre. I imagined it the Minotaur of Greek myth, and I named my picture 'Labyrinth'. I brought out the shapes I saw in the glass by a collage of tinted papers and foils on the back; then the work was framed.

1 Look through the streaky opalescent sheets at your stockists. Choose one which fascinates you – you need not necessarily have decided on its theme at that moment, but if you look at it frequently you will begin to realise how to enhance its most intriguing features.

2 Work out your way of framing the sheet. You might wish to trim some areas, and it will need a hardboard backing to make it less fragile. Having decided how you will do it, leave the framing till last.

3 Using a black felt-tip pen, draw outlines on the surface of the glass according to your interpretation of the shapes you see.

4 Lay a sheet of tracing paper on the glass and trace through all the shapes you have indicated.

5 Cut out these shapes and use as templates from which to cut your coloured papers and other backing materials. It is up to you to use your imagination and incorporate not only papers and foils but visual images, graphics, photos, materials in your collage which will back your panel.

6 Your problem is to place the backing materials in exactly the right position to enhance the shapes in the glass. I found the most accurate way was to fix the smaller pieces on the back of the glass with a tiny dab of fine glue. Then I applied the pieces in layers, finishing with a piece of gold foil which completely backed the entire piece of glass. Keep checking, as you stick, that

fig. 54 Greek Islands commission, showing Crete panel (courtesy *Oxford Mail* and *Times*)

you are placing the modifying materials in the right place.

7 Back with hardboard and frame; but allow some tolerance as the non-machine-made glass could be slightly uneven.

CHAPTER TEN

The history of stained glass

THE BEGINNINGS

It is an impossible task to outline adequately the history of stained glass in one short chapter; but I hope that this sketch of development in Britain, set in a European context – and beyond, in this century – will whet your appetite to read up the subject in depth with the help of the bibliography (p. 116) and stir you to make visits to notable stained glass of every period.

In the last 20 years, stained glass has become an umbrella term for so many different ways of using coloured glass, but it is important for the enthusiast who has become involved in making items, maybe for home decoration, to understand and appreciate how the use of coloured glass has evolved in Western culture, so that when the medium is seen in perspective, all its different facets can be viewed as parts of a rich whole.

The practical necessity of filling window apertures with a protective sheeting was often solved in the late Roman world by the use of translucent alabaster. Examples of this were in the churches of Constantinople in Justinian's time, and in those of Ravenna – and can still be seen in San Vitale, for instance. By the eighth century we know that pieces of coloured glass were being glazed into small openings of ecclesiastical buildings.

It is documented by the Venerable Bede that Benedict Biscop, in AD 680, invited makers of glass from Gaul to come and glaze the windows of his monastic buildings in Monkwearmouth (Sunderland); and archaeological evidence has recently supported this in the find of coloured glass fragments on the site and at the joint foundation at Jarrow. Some of these pieces have now been glazed into a simple panel on view at Jarrow Hall Museum, their date being assessed as seventh- or eighth–century.

The origins of stained glass are obscure: we can only make suggestions regarding how it began. Enamel (as used to decorate caskets, reliquaries and jewellery) is made out of ground glass; and it could well be that the technique of stained glass – creating a structure of coloured glass pieces held together by lead strips – evolved from the technique of cloisonné enamel (coloured enamels held in areas surrounded by strips of metal [cloisons]), a miniaturised form of the stained glass method of construction. We might trace the beginnings of stained glass to the combining of the skills of glaziers and enamellers. It is known that the enamellers who had inherited the Byzantine tradition moved from Venice and settled in Limoges, France, in the late tenth century.

THE ELEVENTH TO THIRTEENTH CENTURIES

When you consider how fragile a medium stained glass is, it is not so surprising that the early stages of development of the art form have disappeared. The powerful Byzantine head of Christ from the Abbey Church of Wissembourg, Alsace, now in the Musée de L'Oeuvre Notre-Dame, Strasbourg, is the earliest intact stained glass head of Christ which has come down to us, dating from the eleventh century. The windows recognised as the oldest surviving are in Augsburg, Bavaria, thought to be from the second half of the eleventh century. Almost certainly from a larger series, five prophets remain, single figures over 2.5m (8ft) tall, romanesque in style. Green, gold and brown predominate; and the faces and drapery details have been boldly glasspainted with pigment – just traced lines. From the head of Christ and these prophets we can surmise that, as they show no lack of technical expertise, there must have been a considerable body of stained glass preceding them. And by the twelfth century the traditional techniques of stained glass were described in a manuscript written by the German monk, Theophilus.

The inspiration for the great Gothic expression of stained glass in France, the most famous examples being Chartres Cathedral and the Sainte Chapelle in Paris, was provided by Abbot Suger (1081–1151) at Saint-Denis on the outskirts of Paris. Contrary to the teaching of the Cistercian order of monks, Abbot Suger believed that beautiful objects in churches were a tribute to the glory of God, not an evil which would distract people from worship. There is no doubt that the magnificent stained glass windows at Saint-Denis (sadly only a fraction have survived) were the stimulus for the thirteenth-century French Gothic windows.

We must now consider why the medieval Church settled on this costly way of expounding the stories of the Christian faith. Light passing through coloured glass has a thrilling effect unmatched by any other medium. The Church taught that light was the symbol of the Divine Spirit: thus transmitted through coloured images on the screen of the windows, it brought a message from heaven. Nowadays, if there is a TV screen transmitting, all eyes go automatically to it; I think that for medieval people, stained glass was just as compelling. They entered the impressive building and their eyes were immediately caught by the visions told through the brilliant windows. The mystery created by vibrant colours and sacred images of divine figures was intended to overwhelm. Remember that most people lived in primitive conditions and their only experience of such colour and splendour would be in religious buildings.

The subjects depicted in the stained glass windows of the medieval period are Christ and the Virgin Mary; the major events in Christ's life; the chief stories of the Old Testament, which were often juxtaposed with Christ's life to show how one event foreshadowed the other (e.g. Abraham sacrificing Isaac relates to God's sacrifice of his only son on the cross), these parallels being known as types and antitypes; the apostles, identified by their emblems; other popular saints, especially local ones, and angels, particularly in the traceries. The details of all these figures were painted on the surface of the glass with a vitreous enamel (pigment) and fired to make permanent. At first, as with the Augsburg Prophets, the glasspainting consisted of traced lines only; and there is a clear similarity between the linear style in glasspainting and that seen in the illuminated books of the period. The dense primary colours of the early glass, so full of impurities, which broke up the light, did not require any more pigment; but as the quality of the glass became more pure, and the colours more translucent, there was need of half-tone to control the light.

Canterbury Cathedral contains the largest range of early glass in England; the choir had to be rebuilt after a fire in 1174, and a major scheme of stained glass windows was made by French craftsmen brought to Canterbury. It depicted the genealogy of Christ: a famous panel is 'Adam Delving'. Around the turn of the century another series of windows was made, a fine example of the medallion type. These windows are divided into panels of different shapes, such as circles or rectangles; they contain scenes (a vivid one is Lot's wife turned into a pillar of salt), and their backgrounds are ornamented with foliage. The colours are the characteristic rich rubies and blues of the period. Much of the glass of the early thirteenth century depicting St Thomas à Becket, the famous martyr who attracted a growing number of pilgrims to his shrine, was destroyed in the Reformation; but some scenes of his miracles still exist.

Medieval glassmaking methods

It is impossible to separate the way stained glass windows were designed and made from the practicalities of the medium. Glass was a precious and expensive material which could not be made in large sheets or on the manufacturing scale we take for granted today. It was all hand-made; and there were two major methods current in medieval times. The first technique was for a gather of glass to be blown into a large bubble which was allowed to sag to form a cylinder shape; it was then opened at one end and cut from the blow iron. This glass cylinder is known as a muff. The muff was then cut from top to bottom and reheated; and in the kiln it would be opened out to a sheet of irregular thickness and colour, with striations, bubbles and particles of unmelted ingredients. (All these 'imperfections' impeded the passage of light through the glass, making the colour glow.) It was allowed to cool slowly; and this process of annealing is essential to all glass, since it cracks if subjected to sudden changes of temperature. The second technique was spun glass: a bubble was blown from a gather of glass and was flattened. It was transferred from the blowpipe to a solid rod called a pontil, held in front of the glory hole of the furnace and spun. As the material became soft in the heat with continuous spinning it would suddenly flash into a disc. It was removed from the rod with its distinctive pontil mark in the centre which, being very thick, was not normally used. Squares or rectangles could be cut from the disc. Nowadays we call spun glass a bullion or roundel: they are much in use for Georgian-type windows. The above two methods are still the ways in which 'antique' hand-made glass is made today.

The problem of glasscutting was another practicality which dictated the appearance of the windows. The shapes had to be kept as simple as possible. The modern glasscutter was not invented until the seventeenth century: the medieval craftsmen shaped the glass pieces in a laborious way. First the outline of the shape to be cut out was painted on the surface of the glass with stale wine or urine, then under this liquid line they ran a hot iron, causing the glass to crack along it. They couldn't depend on this line cracking accurately, so when they got an approximate shape out they made the final adjustments with a special tool called a grozing iron.

The stained glass window of the early period was a mosaic of small pieces held together by a mesh of lead lines. From the beginning, the decorative quality of these lead lines was an integral part of the total effect. The windows were made up of a number of panels held to a 'scaffolding' of ironwork by lead ties or wedges. The ironwork designed by the glazier had to follow the major shapes in the panel so as not to spoil a design, such as going across a head, which would ruin its effect.

The colours which were first made were rich blues (still known as French blue), golds, greens, browns – known as pot metals. From early on glassmakers learned to produce a 'flashed' ruby, as red glass was too dense; instead they fused a layer of ruby glass onto a white base glass. This had the special advantage of being able to be abraded – the red surface laboriously rubbed away to reveal the white underneath – a technique that was to be developed extensively in heraldry at a later date. Buildings which were completely glazed with coloured glass thus represented not only countless thousands of man-hours of skilled craftsmanship, but also money. Chartres Cathedral is an outstanding example of this kind of conspicuous consumption; for it declared the riches lavished by the faithful on a building in honour of the Virgin Mary, whose tunic was the sacred relic miraculously saved from fire which the bejewelled cathedral enshrined. Thus it became a place of pilgrimage, a thriving community; and still is a place of pilgrimage for devotees of stained glass today.

However, a simpler and less costly formula for glazing windows was developed in the thirteenth century, consisting of plain glass painted with foliage, the areas in between finely cross-hatched to break up the light into a beautiful silvery haze: this style is known as 'grisaille' (to make grey). There were little focal points of ruby glass, such as the centre of a flower; and, as the style matured, the trellis effect of branches had recognisable leaves – oak, maple, ivy for instance in Merton College Chapel, Oxford, which also has a band of coloured glass figures and small medallions.

The 'Five Sisters' window in York Minster is the largest and most famous example of this style.

THE FOURTEENTH CENTURY

In the early fourteenth century the use of oxide of silver was discovered, opening up possibilities of a new decorative technique. If this substance was applied to the back of the glass (leaving the front for the pigment) and fired, it turned the glass a tone of yellow, from the palest lemon to the deepest tawny brown-gold, according to how much was applied, the heat of the kiln and the nature of the glass. We see a great exploitation of silver stain in the fourteenth century, in decorating hair, crowns, haloes, garments, canopies etc. It meant that a yellow colour could be used on white glass without the need for a lead line. All yellow areas before the early fourteenth century are pot metal and have a lead line round them. The ethereal effects of stain can be seen in the superb glasspainted panels of the Virgin and Child, the two prioresses and St John the Evangelist in a lower band of the east window, done by the Thomas of Oxford Workshop in the early fifteenth century, in Merton College Chapel, Oxford.

The development of medieval stained glass runs parallel with the developments in Gothic architecture. As masons mastered the art of supporting the vault with pillars, so that the roof did not depend on thick walls with small windows, and as the flying buttress system evolved, so did the possibility of larger and larger window openings with more and more decorated traceries. The windows required overall designs which would convincingly fill the areas, yet not be too expensive. The formula of a single holy figure in a decorated niche (canopy) echoing the architectural motifs in stone and woodcarving became very popular; the canopied surround in which the figure stood could all be less-expensive white glass, painted and stained; and this had the effect of lightening the whole building. The mystery of the blue/ruby colour schemes of the twelfth and thirteenth centuries gave way to the white and gold effect, mixed with a wider range of pot metals: pinks, mauves (mulberry), olive greens. Examples of virtuoso windows of huge size are at York Minster (the Great West Window, 1338); and the Great East Window in Gloucester Cathedral, celebrating the victory of Crecy, 1356. These windows present an overwhelming barrage of holy figures, tier upon tier, compelling the beholder to bow down to the spiritual realm they symbolise.

THE FIFTEENTH CENTURY

York has the richest collection of medieval stained glass

fig. 55 'Virgin and Child': mid-fourteenth-century; the
Latin Chapel, Christ Church Cathedral, Oxford
(reproduced by permission of the Dean and Chapter)

fig. 56 'The Corporal Acts of Mercy: Visiting the Prisoners in the Stocks': early fifteenth-century (reproduced by permission of the Vicar of All Saints, North Street, York)

of all English cities; and in the Minster and many nearby parish churches we can follow the development of glasspainting techniques from simple bold traced lines, to the use of half-tone (sometimes termed 'smear' by art historians, an unfortunate term suggesting messiness – I would prefer the term 'wash' for an unbadgered tone) echoing the traced lines to add emphasis (fourteenth-century) to the development of a fluent and expressive tracing style and subtle working out of smooth matts. It is interesting to note that, as most stained glass is way up above eye-level, certain painting conventions arose to signify the eyes, nose, lips, ears. It is akin to large advertisements on hoardings – when you are close to them you can see only a kind of bold shorthand; but when you stand back, the whole picture coheres. If you use binoculars to study the glass closely (which I recommend to appreciate detail), a fourteenth-century eye is signified by two lines for the lid, a black circle for the iris/pupil and a straight black line under it to show the lower lid. A fifteenth-century eye, however, shows far more sense of form: there are several delicate lines both above and below the actual eye, and this is depicted as a black circle (pupil) with a ring round it (iris). The art of glasspainting is ex-emplified in the many scenes of figure-groups in the Great East Window, York Minster, carried out by John Thornton of Coventry and his team in the short space of three years, 1405–8. This astounding window has as its major theme scenes from the Apocalypse. Equally fascinating, but on a smaller scale, are the stained glass windows in the Church of All Saints, North Street, York. One shows the six Corporal Acts of Mercy – there is a marvellously graphic scene of the Good Man visiting a row of men with their feet in the stocks; another window is based on an early medieval poem, 'The Prikke of Conscience', prophesying the events which will occur on the last fifteen days of the world (such as the sea bursting into flames, rocks and stones burning – alarmingly relevant imagery for today). These windows date from about 1425.

Another famous 'doom' (judgement day, end of the world) window is at Fairford Parish Church, Gloucestershire, where a complete glazing scheme of the very late medieval period still exists. Although the windows have inevitably suffered damage (including a storm which blew out the Great West Window – the top part in particular is much restored) the lower right-hand area still clearly shows some gruesome devils in hell devouring the souls of the wicked. Elsewhere in the church's windows the direction of sixteenth-century glass is appearing: figures glasspainted with tones to create form; perspective; vistas – all bringing a three-dimensional aspect into stained glass which, up to this time, had been a very much two-dimensional medium showing figures from a sacred world. This commission, if not carried out by Low Countries craftsmen, is strongly influenced by new trends from that part of Europe.

THE SIXTEENTH CENTURY

We see the new spirit of the Renaissance in the major stained glass commissions of the sixteenth century: 26 windows for King's College Chapel, Cambridge, carried out in the years 1515–17 and 1526–31. They exemplify the changes that were taking place in art and religion. The Renaissance world is very much present in these windows: in the depiction of costume and architecture this is not the visionary world of beyond, but a celebration of the actual material world. The glasspainting is strong, bold, modelled. There is a foreground, a middle ground and a background in many scenes, reminiscent of easel painting. Stained glass is losing the characteristics of the medium and becoming dominated by pictorial values, which lasted through until past the eighteenth century. The commission is well documented, so we know that most of the designs were by an Antwerp designer, Vellert; and a Dutchman, Bernard Flower, the King's Glazier, carried out four windows of the first period. After his death, Galyon Hone, another Dutchman, succeeded him, with a team of craftsmen, some of whom were English. They were responsible for the 22 remaining windows.

fig. 57 'Triumph of Chastity': early sixteenth-century roundel in Wilton Parish Church, near Salisbury shows superb glasspainting and staining marred by an insensitive glazing bar (reproduced by permission of the Vicar)

In the 1530s the Reformation shook England: the dissolution of the monasteries caused terrible damage to church furnishings, including stained glass. Reformers of the sixteenth century thought that images of religious personages, whether in stone, wood or whatever medium, seduced mankind from serious contemplation of God; so Christians were exhorted to turn away from any colourful depictions of religious subjects.

From the sixteenth century onwards, the traditions of stained glass, in particular the techniques of glasspainting, were continued in the many thousands of small domestic roundels and panels produced in the Low Countries, Switzerland and Germany. The subjects of these panels were often based on woodcuts and engravings of the period; some of them are devotional, but many show classical scenes, allegories or the seasons. Heraldic panels became very popular as moneyed families were determined to assert their status – these panels were often made to celebrate the marriage of two important families. In these panels, especially the Swiss ones, we see the use of coloured enamels applied to the surface and fired; so changes of colour could be effected without lead lines. This development was to increase the growing tendency to treat a stained glass panel as a branch of easel painting, rather than a technique in its own right. The use of coloured enamels painted onto the glass was to be the major characteristic of stained glass from the late sixteenth to the early nineteenth century; but enamels tend to flake, and their opacity destroys the translucent quality which had been the great beauty of medieval glass.

THE SEVENTEENTH AND EIGHTEENTH CENTURIES

The technique of enamel-painting on glass received a strong impetus in the seventeenth century because of the actual unavailability of coloured glass. In 1633 King Louis XIII invaded Lorraine, the district which had many glasshouses where pot metals were produced; by 1636 he ordered the entire area to be devastated. It seems that the art of making coloured glass was virtually lost for about 100 years, for Britain always imported coloured glass from the Continent.

Oxford has a notable collection of seventeenth-century stained glass because of its connections with Archbishop Laud and the Court. The Archbishop patronised the van Linge brothers, Bernard and Abraham, glasspainters from Emden. Bernard's East Window in Wadham College Chapel, dated 1622, is an interesting balance of stained glass foreground figures and delicately enamelled Flemish-style vistas; but the robust style of Abraham can be seen in the Cathedral of Christ Church in the window 'Jonah Contemplating Nineveh', (1630s). Only the red and blue of Jonah's garments are coloured glass; all the yellows (the decorative gourds, the sun etc.) are richly stained; and the right-hand light is entirely enamelled, showing houses spectacularly perched on the hillside. His bold glasspainting style is akin to theatrical scene-painting in its bravura, and can also be seen in characterful commissions in Balliol College and the entire chapel (excluding the East Window) of University College, 1641. The onset of the Civil War drove these artists out of England; and during those years much more destruction of stained glass was carried out by zealots.

During the Restoration, when monied people began to require craftsmanship in glass again, stained glass artists began to advertise themselves. Henry Gyles of York (1645–1709) undertook large windows, but became known for the novelty of stained glass sundials.

The eighteenth century admired the classical forms of art; and this change of taste was responsible for much destruction of medieval glass. In New College Chapel, Oxford, you can study four commissions, all enamelled with a predominate grid of leading. William Price the Younger 'restored' the Thomas Glazier late fourteenth-century windows on the south side of the main chapel, 1735–40. He retains the design of single figures under canopies – in fact he actually reglazes a considerable amount of medieval glass in the canopy areas – but his portly figures of archbishops and saints have all the mannered gestures of the Baroque: they project from heavily-painted niches, and the glass is considered as a canvas on which to paint a picture which is spoilt by the technical necessity of a grid of lead lines. This applies to the other eighteenth-century work in the Chapel. The two windows nearest the altar on the north side are painted with a tawny pigment and were once in the West Window. They were carried out by Peckitt of York in 1765 but demoted by new glass in 1783. He also enamelled the three remaining windows on the north side. They are beautifully executed (see the Twelve Tribes badge on Aaron's breast), with attractive tones of apricot and mauve, and the faces are all flesh-tinted with rosy lips and blue eyes. But they were undoubtedly designed to upset the Fellows of the College – there are chinoiserie pagodas, so fashionable at the time; and also note that Eve was robed in Victorian times – you can see her skirt of fig leaves sticking out from an enveloping garment.

The Great West Window originally contained a Jesse Tree of the late fourteenth century by Thomas Glazier. When Peckitt was commissioned to make a new window, he was forced to take the old glass in part payment; and, as he was in charge of restoration in

fig. 58 'The Epiphany': one of a set of nine windows; complete glazing scheme by Henry Holiday, 1864, made by Lavers and Barraud, Worcester College Chapel, Oxford; (reproduced by permission of the Provost and Fellows)

York Minster, Oxford's loss is York's gain, for luckily this glass was saved and can be seen in the Minster today. In 1783 Peckitt's work was ousted by the highly fashionable painter, Reynolds, who produced oil paintings, not stained glass cartoons, for his glasspainter, Jervais, to work from. The window is carried out with a high degree of skill: the lower range depicts The Virtues (fashionable ladies sat for them); the upper part is a Nativity based on a painting by Correggio; but the window is entirely opaque and the very virtue of glass, its translucency, is in abeyance.

However, in the second half of the eighteenth century, partly due to Walpole's example at Strawberry Hill, Twickenham, the taste for the Gothic and the medieval was revived, and with it an interest in the roundels and small panels produced in the previous centuries. Walpole had a large collection; and so it became fashionable for English tourists to bring back quantities at a cheap price and have them glazed either

into their mansions or into local churches. In fact the expert on this subject, Dr William Cole, thinks that there are probably more panels surviving in England than on the Continent, thanks to this fashion. A collection can be seen at the National Trust house, Felbrigg Hall, Norfolk; at Waterperry House, Wheatley, Oxfordshire (owned by a private college); and in parish churches such as Rownhams, near Southampton, Addington in Buckinghamshire, and Malpas, Cheshire.

THE NINETEENTH CENTURY

The nineteenth-century stained glass revival is inseparable from the rediscovery of the Gothic style of architecture, and the huge and unabating demand for windows in the countless churches, colleges, public buildings, mansions and smaller domestic buildings supported by the wealth of the British Empire. It became fashionable for memorial windows to be donated, so the Church could rely on benefactions in stained glass. This demand caused many stained glass studios to be set up during the Victorian era, often employing a large number of craftsmen and apprentices. In the International Exhibition of 1862 there were 28 stained glass firms offering work in every style. A parallel movement in France and Germany created many new windows and a revival of ancient techniques.

Early commissions, in the 1840s, suffered from harsh colours of glass – unsubtle blues, rubies, yellows, greens – which are characteristic of this period, and can be seen in the Gothic-style windows of Hardman-Pugin and Wailes of Newcastle. The great improvement in the colour and range of glass available is due to the studies of Charles Winston, a barrister who had a passion for stained glass. He published a carefully-considered and painstakingly-illustrated commentary and survey in 1847; and, through his analyses of medieval glass, helped by Dr Medlock of the Royal College of Chemistry, enabled Powell's glassworks to manufacture superb glass which made a major contribution to the aesthetic effect of windows from the late 1850s, especially the William Morris Studio's commissions, which always used Powell's glass.

A studio set up in 1855–6, Clayton and Bell, produced the most consistent level of design and craftsmanship in the reinterpretation of medieval styles till the end of the century; and you can study the change in fashion from twelfth- to sixteenth-century-based styles in Exeter College Chapel, Oxford, a building designed by Scott and inspired by the Sainte Chapelle in Paris. The apse windows are bright blues, rubies, yellows and greens, based on thirteenth-century groups and canopies (1859–61); the windows on the south side become progressively more Renaissance in style, with richer glass from Chance of Birmingham, 1860s. On the north side are commissions of the 1870s and '80s employing chiaroscuro, dramatic scenes and heavy glasspainting with oil matts.

The studio set up by William Morris and partners in 1861 was determined not to be dominated by medieval models: their period of inspiration was the pre-Raphaelite art of Italy. There are four Morris commissions in the Cathedral of Christ Church, Oxford, all designed by Burne-Jones; and an early window by the designer, made by Powell in 1859. Starting with the early work, it is a distinctive commission both in design and tapestry of rich colour showing crowded scenes of the lives of the patron saint, Frideswide. The bold glasspainting is fresh and lively; particularly eye-catching is the ship of souls in the tracery circle. In 1870 Morris & Co. carried out 'Faith, Hope and Charity': three symbolic female figures, of which Hope is very much a Botticelli figure in her flowing graceful garments. The Saint Cecilia window (1875) in the east end has the same grace; and, as is clearly demonstrated by the cartoons by Burne-Jones for the St Catherine commission (1878), which are on view in the Chapter House, the artist produced superb elegant drawings. They were, however, drawings, not stained glass cartoons, and this explains the glaringly ugly lead lines of these 1870s windows, which were superimposed on the drawing, and not thought out at the design stage. When the figures are clad in white, these lead lines obtrude particularly; they also mar the otherwise beautiful window, the Vyner Memorial (1872–3), depicting three young prophets with their amazing red bullion haloes, silhouetted against a deep green foliage background. In the 1880s Morris began to make the leading an integral part of the design (as in the Birmingham Cathedral windows, 1885) which gives rhythm and unity to the composition.

The Morris Studio also carried out many smaller domestic panels for private houses; in the Green Drawing Room (1867) at the Victoria and Albert Museum, London, a total decor is preserved – the stained glass depicting delicate scenes of single figures entitled 'Garland Weavers'. An earlier series of six panels, telling the story of St George, with a much more robust glasspainting style (1862), can also be seen at the museum; various other panels are also in their collection, and at Birmingham City Art Gallery too. These panels remind us that alongside the thriving ecclesiastical market was a demand for decoration of the home, a tradition which was to continue through the Victorian era, with its penchant for medieval scenes and heraldic motifs, to the flowing lines of the Art Nouveau. Any Edwardian house of any pretension would expect to have some embellishment in stained glass in door, top casement and staircase windows, right through to the many small 1920s and early '30s houses with their Art Deco motifs in door and window panels. Of course, much of this work was not individually designed. There were local glaziers with pattern books from which you could select your own permutations of what was on offer. But at least all this choice kept the medium in front of the public's eye and maintained its currency.

In the second half of the nineteenth century, large studios such as Clayton and Bell, Morris and Co., Kempe, and Powell all had craftsmen and apprentices numbering over 100, and a strict hierarchy was obtained. At the top were the designers; than came the glasspainters: the foreman painter concentrated on heads and hands; groups were busy on drapery, calligraphy, architectural borders; and the apprentices often worked on the traceries. Then there were teams of cutters, glaziers, cementers and fixers. It explains why some studios achieved a virtuoso level of accomplishment similar to a great symphony orchestra: I would single out Kempe's studio in particular. In the last two decades of the century his studio produced labour-intensive commissions, often in the fifteenth-century style, and German-influenced: his figures wore richly-diapered robes, painted with encrustations of pearls. A typical commission is the West Window in Burford church, Oxon. There was the most highly-wrought glasspainting: oil matts, acid-etching, quilling, staining; but it overreached itself and led to the reaction early this century when white glass began to predominate and ligher colours to be the fashion.

The kind of mass-production methods which this type of large studio inevitably used gave rise to a more individualistic approach, the Arts and Crafts Movement, characterised by the artist-craftsman Whall, who had a great influence on his many students. He was horrified that the big studios would repeat their designs many times in different churches; he urged that every stained glass artist should be able to design, paint, and at least know all about cutting and glazing, so that the work they produced should have a personal touch.

TIFFANY AND ART NOUVEAU IN THE USA

Tiffany is a major name associated with Art Nouveau in the USA. He spent a fortune on producing different types of novelty glass, especially milky opalescents and mottles, so that the fascination of the glass was the great attraction of his imaginative windows and lamps. The lamp base and shade were designed as an artistic entity: the borders of the shade decorated with sinuous foliage, fruit clusters or flowers. These intricate, curving shapes

fig. 59 'Chaucer Asleep': from a series of panels by William Morris, 1864 (reproduced by permission of the Victoria and Albert Museum)

could not be assembled with lead calm as it was not delicate enough, so the metal channelling developed for these lamps was the forerunner of the copperfoil so useful nowadays in making three-dimensional items.

DEVELOPMENTS IN OUR CENTURY

This century has seen a great divergence of styles and techniques, according to the demands of the commis-

sion. Work for historic cathedrals and churches can require a fastidiously-executed reinterpretation of medieval styles. Comper, Webb and Easton are essentially in that tradition – their windows all let in much more light than Victorian work for they are on white backgrounds, but the tracing and painting is in the highest tradition of craftsmanship. The Air Force memorial window in Westminster Abbey (carried out by Hugh Easton just after the war), known as 'The Battle of Britain Window', is a notable example. Modern buildings, however, demand contemporary stained glass, and the best-known commissions equalling their architectural setting are those in Coventry Cathedral, rebuilt after the Second World War. The large work which is immediately eye-catching is the

Baptistry window, designed by the artist John Piper and made by Reyntiens and team. It is so bold an image – light emerging from darkness – that it is a great teaching window in the medieval tradition. The leaded rectangular panels are set in a large grid of stonework; the glasspainting is broad, textured, in keeping with the style and scale. The nave windows cannot be seen until you reach the altar and turn round: then, as you walk down the cathedral, the pairs of windows tell the story of Christian themes and mankind's spiritual life, symbolised by different colours and semi-abstract images. They were designed and made at the Royal College of Art by Lawrence Lee, assisted by Geoffrey Clarke and Keith New.

War damage in Germany gave the Catholic Church there a great impetus to discover a formula for providing new stained glass windows which were modern in imagery yet economically viable. The technique of glasspainting was dispensed with, for it is a time-consuming technique which doubles the cost of a commission. Various artists since the 1950s have produced striking windows employing lead lines in rhythmic patterns, combined with a controlled use of coloured glass. The chief protagonists of this style are Meistermann, Schaffrath, Buschulte and Schreiter. The best of these commissions have attracted attention from all over the world.

The artist Chagall has produced designs for stained glass commissions in various places, some of the largest being for the synagogue of the Hadassah-Hebrew University Medical Centre, Jerusalem, 1962. There are several commissions in England, including Chichester Cathedral and Tudely Church, Kent. Chagall's figures float in richly-coloured amorphous backgrounds in both his paintings and his stained glass designs. But the problem of the lead lines, such a bugbear to the eighteenth century, play no integral part in Chagall's designs: although richly satisfying in colour, the aesthetics of the lead lines are not solved.

After the Second World War, France developed the technique of dalle-de-verre set in concrete, and many churches, especially modern ones, contain this bold modern technique, which can be kept abstract or used figuratively. A fine example of its figurative use is at Buckfast Abbey, Devon: the East Window of the Chapel of the Blessed Sacrament displays a majestic figure of Christ with outstretched hands standing by a Eucharist table. The thick slabs of glass (dalles) have been shaled (chipped in a decorative way) to create facets, and set in frames of concrete which themselves create a decorative pattern. This work was carried out by the monks under the leadership of Dom Charles Norris, O.S.B.

Individual stained glass artists who have been in the tradition of Whall's ideals, aiming at a very personal approach and determined to carry out the bulk of the work themselves, have contributed unique work to twentieth-century stained glass. Two Irish exponents were Harry Clarke and Evie Hone: their styles are an absolute contrast and show how flexible the medium is when used with personal vision. Harry Clarke (1889–1931) produced highly-wrought, jewel-like windows and panels incorporating the virtuoso use of glasspainting and acid-etching; his style was very close to Beardsley's. Evie Hone (1893–1951) was a painter trained in Paris in the 1920s. She was influenced by Rouault and the religious imagery of early Irish sculpture, and this primitivism is powerfully demonstrated in her best-known work in England: the East Window of Eton College Chapel, Berks. Ervin Bossanyi (1891–1975), a Hungarian exiled to England from 1934 onwards, whose working methods I was privileged to watch from 1960 onwards, also produced a small corpus of inspired work, among the finest being 'Angel Blessing the Washerwomen' at the Tate Gallery, London; the four windows in Canterbury Cathedral (1956–60) and the Washington Cathedral commission, USA. In Canterbury Cathedral the artist was given a free hand in offering a subject dear to his heart and his own experience. Having been interned in the First World War, he used his memories to create one great window, 'Salvation', which depicts a prisoner being freed by an angel and welcomed by his family; the other is 'Peace': God the Father blessing the children of all nations. These windows are rich in colour, their themes are clearly depicted, and these vast areas of glass are all handpainted by the artist himself in his inimitable style.

It has to be admitted that where there are clients, public or private, willing to pay money for stained glass, there the momentum will be. Every artform needs the manure of investment before it can flourish. Germany, USA, Canada, Japan and Australia are all fertile places for stained glass to develop today because there are plenty of patrons willing to pay for the medium in all kinds of settings, such as churches, libraries, hospitals, hotels, restaurants and private houses. Sadly, this is not the case in Britain, although there is no lack of talent or expertise.

Everyone whose interest in stained glass is awakened by making simple panels and decorative items, has a chance to contribute to the appreciation and continuation of the art by taking an interest in the heritage of stained glass in their local area; by supporting its use to enliven any setting; and by attempting to emulate the highest standards in their own work, no matter how simple. In this way they may feel part of a medium which has a limitless potential.

fig. 60 'Healing' from the Dr Julius Commission, artist's
version, 1932 (reproduced by permission of Mr Jo
Bossanyi, the artist's son)

HEALTH AND SAFETY

Since the First Edition of my book in 1985, E.E.C. Health and Safety Regulations have come into force in connection with using noxious substances in the workplace. I recommend the following Health and Safety Procedures be carried out by all persons, professional or amateur.

Soldering the Panel (page 23)
When preparing your panel prior to soldering, lead oxidises, so you must clean your leads at the joins. When doing this, fine lead particles are raised, so you should wear a suitable mask for protection. The proper mask is called a Premium Particulate Respirator 8835, which guards against fumes and dust particles (see List of Suppliers). Fitting must be close to the face to be effective. The soldering process itself also produces fumes, which should not be inhaled. The mask described above should be worn for your protection.

Glasspainting (page 39)
The pigment used in glasspainting is finely-ground glass with iron oxide and lead. Recently people have become aware of the implications of breathing this fine material. Sensible precautions should be taken when using it. It is recommended that the Premium Particulate Respirator mask definitely be worn when removing highlights (see p 44) as a fine dust rises when the dry pigment is removed with stiff brushes. If you wish to exercise great caution, you might choose to wear your mask during all the processes of glasspainting.

Assembling a Two-dimensional Item (page 64).
When you are soldering, a Premium Particulate Respirator 8835 mask should be used at all times.

Bibliography

History of stained glass and major historical craft books

ADAM, Stephen *Decorative Stained Glass: 1855–1931* Academy Editions 1980

ANGUS, Mark *Modern Stained Glass in British Churches* Mowbray 1984

ARMITAGE, E. Liddel *Stained Glass* Leonard Hill 1959

BAKER, John *English Stained Glass of the Medieval Period* Thames and Hudson 1978

COWAN, Painton *Rose Windows* Thames and Hudson 1979

DAY, Lewis F. *Windows . . . about stained and painted glass* Batsford 1897

GIBSON, Peter *The Stained and Painted Glass of York Minster* (handguide) Jarrold Publications, Norwich, for the Dean and Chapter of York Minster 1981

HARRIES, John *Discovering Stained Glass* (pocketbook) Shire Publications 1968

HARRISON, Martin *Victorian Stained Glass* Barrie and Jenkins 1980

LE COUTER, J. D. *English Medieval Painted Glass,* 1926, republished by SPCK 1978

LEE, Lawrence *The Appreciation of Stained Glass* Oxford University Press 1977

LEE, SEDDON & STEPHENS *Stained Glass* Mitchell Beazley 1974

OSBORNE, June *Stained Glass in England* Muller 1981

PIPER, John *Stained Glass: Art or Anti-art?* Studio Vista 1968

SAN CASCIANI, Paul *The Stained Glass of Oxford* (handguide) P.S.C. Stained Glass Activities, Oxford, 1982

SEWTER, A. Charles *The Stained Glass of William Morris and his Circle* (two vols) Paul Mellon Centre for Studies in British Art, Yale University Press, Newhaven/London 1974

SOWERS, Robert *Stained Glass– An Architectural Art* Zwemmer 1965

WHALL, C. H. *Stained Glass Work* John Hogg 1905

WINSTON, Charles *An Inquiry into the difference of style observable in Ancient Glass Painting . . . by an amateur* (two vols) Parker, Oxford 1847

WOODFORDE, Christopher *English Stained and Painted Glass* Clarendon Press Oxford 1954

Current craft instruction books

DUNCAN, Alastair *The Technique of Leaded Glass* Batsford 1975

ELSKUS, Albinas *The Art of Painting on Glass* Charles Scribner's Sons, New York 1980

FROBIETER-MUELLER, Jo *Practical Stained Glass Craft* David and Charles 1984

ISENBERG, Anita and Seymour *How to Work in Stained Glass* Chilton Book Company, USA (2nd edn) 1983

LUCIANO and COLSON *Stained Glass Lamp Art* Hidden House, USA 1976

O'BRIEN, Vincent *Techniques of Stained Glass* Studio Vista 1977

REYNTIENS, Patrick *The Technique of Stained Glass* Batsford 1967

ROTHENBERG, Polly *The Complete Book of Creative Glass Art* Allen and Unwin 1974

Suppliers

SUPPLIERS (UK)

Stained Glass Materials and Tools

Jennifer Jane Glass Studio
Abbey Studio
Fintray
ABERDEEN AB2 0JB
Tel: 01224 791363

Harwil Marketing
Unit 20B
Connswater Industrial Estate
East Bread Street
BELFAST BT4 1AN
Northern Ireland
01232 732311/2

Birmingham Stained Glass
100–102 Edward Road
Balsall Heath
BIRMINGHAM
Tel: 0121 440 0909

Bournemouth Stained Glass
790 Wimbourne Road
Moordown
BOURNEMOUTH
Tel: 01202 514734

Cambridge Stained Glass
8 George Street
Willingham
CAMBRIDGE CB4 5LJ
Tel: 01954 60301

Broadland Stained Glass
30 Riverside Road
GORLESTON-ON-SEA
Norfolk NR31 6PU
Tel/fax: 01493 443431

Cheshire Glass Company
Banbury Street
Lower Hillgate
STOCKPORT
Cheshire SK1 3AR
Tel: 0161 480 1873

Creative Glass
140D Redland Road
Redland
BRISTOL BS6 6YA
Tel: 01272 737025

Decorative Glass Supplies Ltd
Dubb Lane
BINGLEY
West Yorks BD16 2NW
Tel: 01274 510633
Fax: 01274 510623

Daedalian Glass Ltd
The Old Smithy
Cold Row
Carr Lane
Stalmine
POULTON-LE-FYLDE
Lancs FY6 9DW
Tel: 01253 702531
Fax: 01253 702532

Edinburgh Stained Glass House
46 Balcarres Street
Morningside
EDINBURGH EH10 5JQ
Tel: 0131 452 8062

Glass Heritage Ltd
Reynolds Warehouse
The Docks
GLOUCESTER GL1 2EN
Tel: 01452 503803

Hetley Stained Glass Suppliers
School House Lane
Stepney
LONDON E1 9JA
Tel: 0171 790 2333
Fax: 0171 790 0201
(Phone enquirers: ask for Hetley)

Irish Stained Glass
Hanoveu Quay
DUBLIN Eire
Tel: 010 3531 773354

IWF Ltd
78A Forsyth Road
NEWCASTLE-UPON-TYNE NE2 3EU
Tel: 0191 281 0945

Kansacraft
The Flour Mill
Wath Road
Elsecar
BARNSLEY South Yorks S74 8HW
Tel: 01226 747424
Fax: 01226 743712

Lead and Light
35A Hartland Road
LONDON NW1 4DB
Tel: 0171 485 0997
Fax: 0171 284 2660

Leaded Glass Lighting
Unit B
Bakers Boatyard
Brickyard Lane
Starcross
EXETER
Devon EX6 8RY
Tel: 01626 891383

Long Eaton Stained Glass
1 Northcote Street
LONG EATON
Notts ND10 1EZ
Tel: 01602 732320

Opus Stained Glass
Old Village Hall
Mill Lane
POYNINGS
West Sussex BN4 7AE
Tel: 0179 156223

Pearsons Glass Ltd
Maddrell Street
LIVERPOOL L3 7EH
Tel: 0151 207 1474

Stained Glass Construction and Design
62 Fairfield Street
LONDON SW18 1DY
Tel: 0181 874 8822

Sunrise Stained Glass
58–60 Middle Street
SOUTHSEA
Hants PO5 4BP
Tel: 01705 750512

Tempsford Stained Glass
The Old School
Tempsford
SANDY
Beds SG19 2AW
Tel: 01767 640235

Brushmakers

A. S. Handover Ltd
37H Mildmay Grove
Islington
LONDON N1 4RH
Tel: 0171 359 4696
Fax: 0171 354 3658

Kilns

Essex Kilns Ltd
Woodrolfe Road
Tollesbury
MALDON
Essex CM9 8SJ
Tel: 01621 869342
Fax: 01621 868522

Laser Kilns Ltd
Unit 9
Crispin Industrial Centre
Angel Road Works
LONDON N18 2DT
Tel: 0181 803 1016
Fax: 0181 807 2888

Masks

8835: For protection against dust and fumes;
9906: For protection against acid fumes:
3M United Kingdom PLC
P.O. Box 1
BRACKNELL
Berks RG12 1JU
Tel: 01344 858000
(ask for the name of your local distributor)

Cement fondue (for glass appliqué)

Tiranti Ltd
27 Warren Street
LONDON W1
Tel: 0171 636 8565

For Suppliers in USA refer to *Stained Glass Quarterly* Magazine (see Stained Glass Association of America)

Contact suppliers for their up-to-date lists of pattern books.
ELSKUS, Albinas *The Art of Painting on Glass* Charles Scribner's Sons, New York 1980
ISENBERG, Anita and Seymour *How to Work in Stained Glass* Chilton Book Company, USA (2nd edition) 1983
LUNDSTROM, Boyce and SCHWOERER, Daniel *Glass Fusing, Book 1* Vitreous Publications Inc Portland Oregon 97202 1983 USA
REYNTIENS, Patrick *The Technique of Stained Glass* Batsford 1967,77

Stained Glass Book Search
Tel/fax: 0117 950 7362

Venables, Morris and Juliet
Antiquarian and Secondhand Books
Buy and sell books on Stained Glass. Catalogue annually.
270 Hensbury Road
BRISTOL BS10 7QR
Tel: 01272 507362

SUPPLIERS (USA)

California
Franciscan Glass Co. Inc.
100 San Antonio Circle
MOUNTAIN VIEW CA 94040

Hollander Glass Inc.
1057a Dale
STANTON CA 90680

Colorado
D & L Stained Glass Supply
4919 N Broadway
BOULDER CO 80302

Florida
Florida Stained Glass Inc.
1510 Capital Circle SE
TALLAHASSEE FL 32301

Illinois
Chicago Art Glass Inc.
2382 United Lane
ELK GROVE VILLAGE IL 60007

Indiana
Kokomo Opalescent Glass Co.
1310 South Market Street
PO Box 2265
KOKOMO IN 46902

Kansas
Talley's Stained Glass Inc.
3054 S 44th St.
KANSAS CITY KS 66106

Minnesota
North County Art Glass Inc.
2125 East Hennepin Ave
MINNEAPOLIS MN 55413

New York
S A Bendheim Co. Inc.
122 Hudson Street
NEW YORK NY 10013

Oregon
Bullseye Glass Co.
3722 Se 21st Ave.
PORTLAND OR 97202

Texas
Houston Stained Glass Supply
1829 Arlington St.
HOUSTON TX 77008

Washington
Spectrum Stained Glass Inc.
PO Box 646
WOOINVILLE WA 98072

Courses

The British Society of Master Glass Painters issues a frequently updated list of educational establishments, Local Authorities and Members holding courses. Please send stamped addressed envelope (essential) to BSMGP (see address under 'Societies') . The following information is taken from that list:

Higher Education offering full-time courses:

Central St. Martin's School of Art and Design
Southampton Row
LONDON WC1B 4AP
Tel: 0171 753 9090

Chelsea School of Art
Manresea Road
LONDON SW3 6LS
Tel: 0171 351 3844

Edinburgh College of Art
Heriot-Watt University
Lauriston Place
EDINBURGH EH3 9DF
Tel: 0131 229 9311

Froebel Institute College
Roehampton Lane
LONDON SW15 5PJ
Tel: 0181 342 3000

Glasgow School of Art
167 Renfrew Street
GLASGOW G3 6RQ
Tel: 0141 353 4500

North East Wales Institute of Higher Education
49 Regent Street
WREXHAM LL13 1PS
Tel: 01978 290666

Royal College of Art
Kensington Gore
LONDON SW7 2EU
Tel: 0171 584 5020

University of Sunderland
School of Art, Design and Communications
Ashburne House
Back House Park
Ryhope Road
SUNDERLAND
Tel: 0191 515 2126

West Glamorgan Institute
Alexandra Road
SWANSEA SA1 5DU
Tel: 01792 481179

Wolverhampton University
School of Art and Design
Molyneux Road
WOLVERHAMPTON WV1 1SB
Tel: 01902 313002

Further, Community and Adult Education

Contact your Local Authority for current details. In London *Floodlight* Magazine publishes details of courses.

Paul San Casciani FMGP holds courses in London, Oxford and elsewhere. Send stamped addressed envelope to:
Paul San Casciani Stained Glass Activities
11 Dale Close
Thames Street
OXFORD OX1 1TU
Tel: 01865 727529

SOCIETIES

The British Society of Master Glass Painters
The Secretary
c/o The Art Workers' Guild
6 Queen Square
LONDON WC1N 3AR

Fellows, Associates, Craft Associates and Ordinary
Members. Recently the BSMGP has established a
national Accreditation Scheme for Studios and
Individuals working in stained glass, to try to uphold
standards and help clients. Holds Spring and Autumn
Lectures followed by supper at The Art Workers'
Guild (open to non-members).

Annual Weekend Conference in different areas:
stained glass tours, lectures, open forum (open to
non-members).

Publications:
Spring and Autumn MAGAZINE (A4, colour cover,
approx 20 pages)
Articles, Members' News, Courses, Suppliers'
Adverts etc.
JOURNAL. Annual scholarly publication. Illustrated.

BSMP regularly updated list available of Stained
Glass Courses held by Higher Education Colleges,
Local Authorities and Individuals (see 'Courses').

The Worshipful Company of Glaziers and
Painters of Glass
Glaziers' Hall
9 Montague Close
London Bridge
LONDON SE1 9DD
Tel: 0171 403 3300
Fax: 0171 407 6036

Holds 3 'Layman's Guide to Glass' Lectures during
the year (open to non-members). Actively promotes
interest in stained glass. Houses The Stained Glass
Repository – a store for glass from redundant
churches, which aims to transfer the windows
to suitable buildings. Holds Stained Glass
Competitions.

National Association of Decorative and Fine Art
Societies
NADFAS House
8 Guildford Street
LONDON WC1N 1DT

NADFAS has published an invaluable Catalogue
of Stained Glass Makers' Marks which can be
purchased from the above address. The Association is
actively encouraging Members to make an inventory
of stained glass in their local parish churches.

The Stained Glass Association of America
Editorial and Administrative Offices
6 SW Second Street
Suite No. 7
LEE'S SUMMIT MO 64063–2352
Tel: (800) 438 9581
Tel: (816) 524 9313
Fax: (186) 524 9405

Very large society, active state by state and nationally.
Regular Conferences.
Quarterly MAGAZINE marketed internationally,
averages 80 pages, well illustrated in colour, lively
articles featuring new commissions, book reviews.
Can be purchased in GB from Hetley Stained Glass
Suppliers (see List of Suppliers p118).

Index